Farting Animals Coloring Book

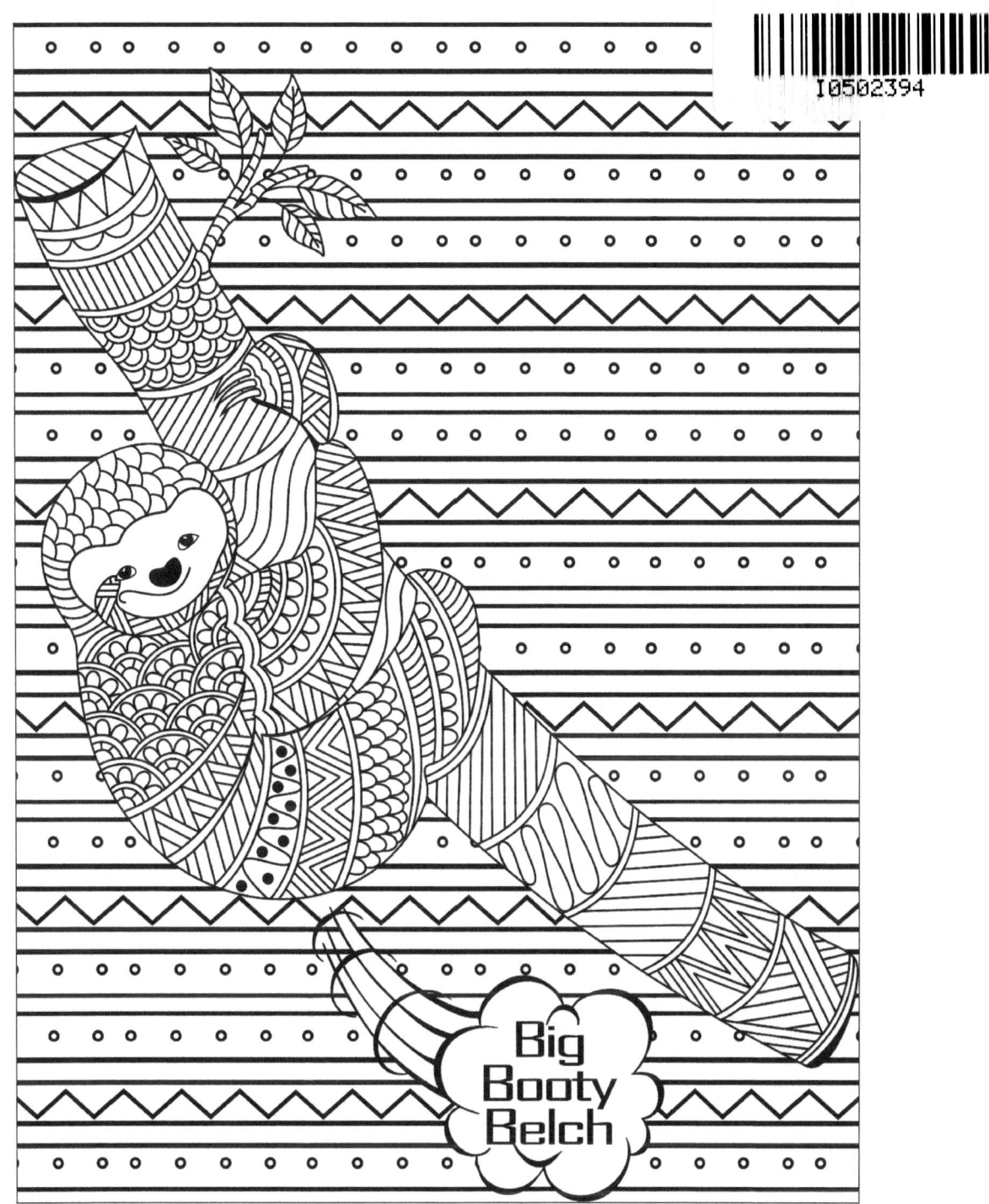

Adults Hilarious Stress Relieving
Farting Coloring Book With 31 Funny Designs

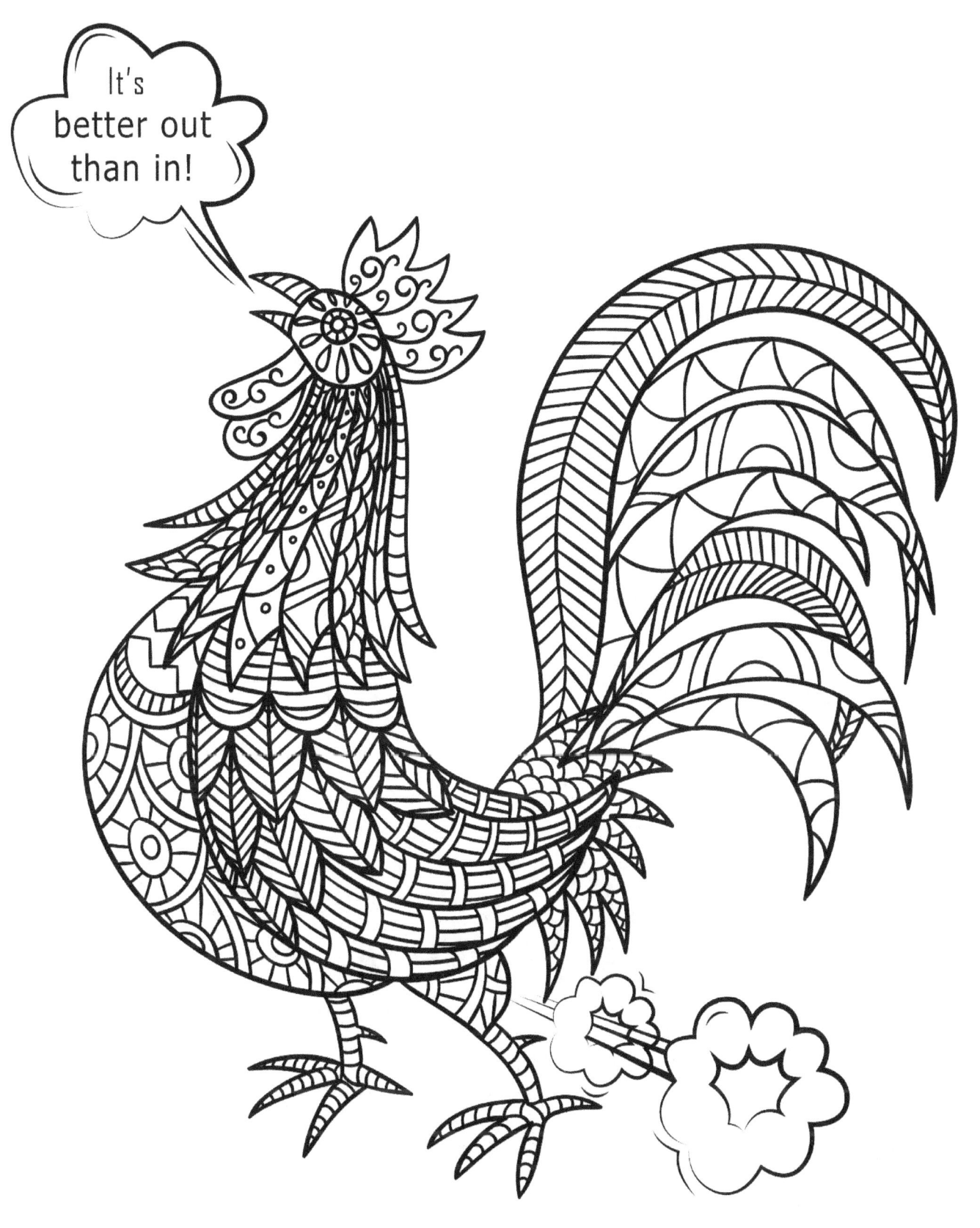

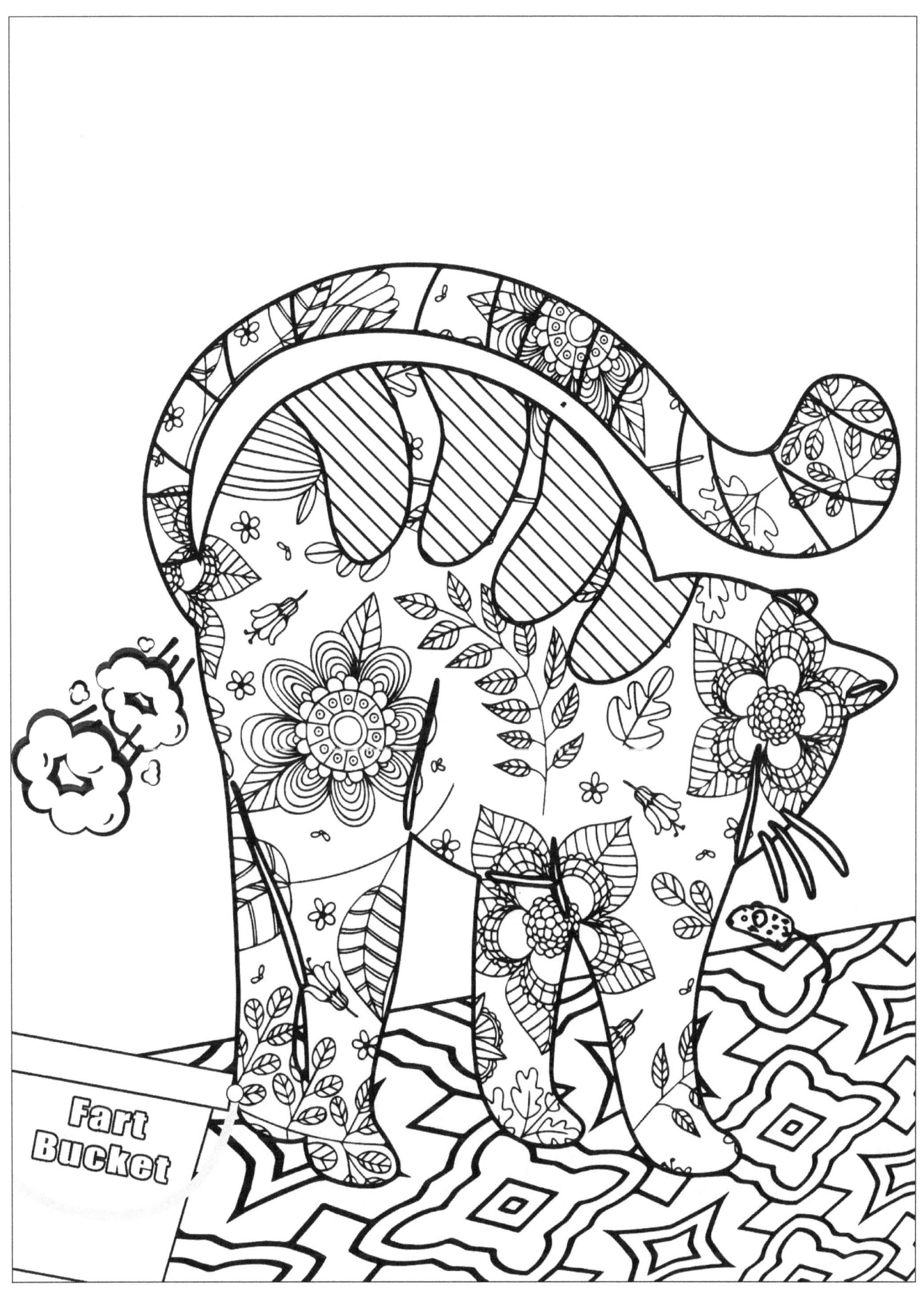

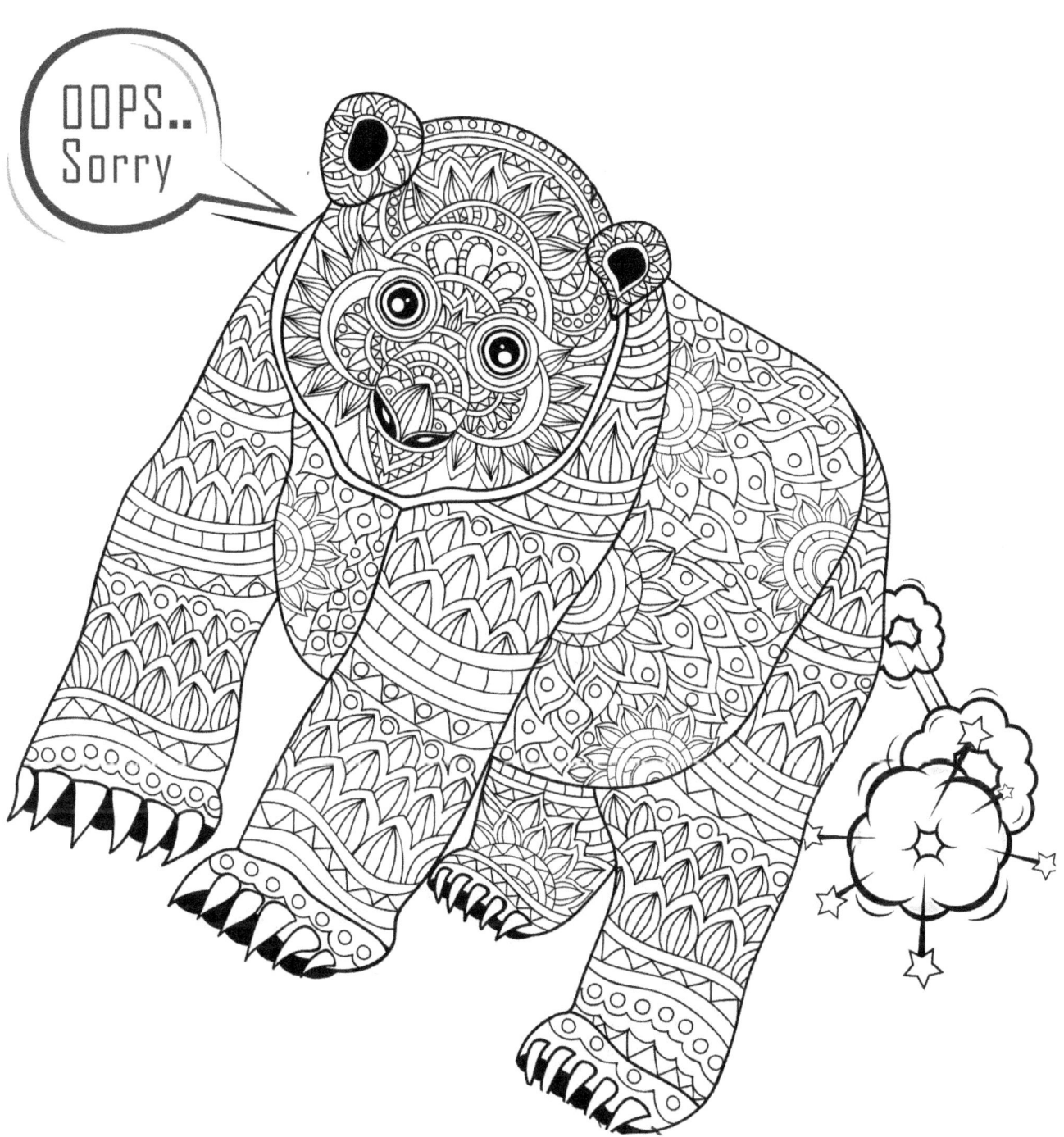

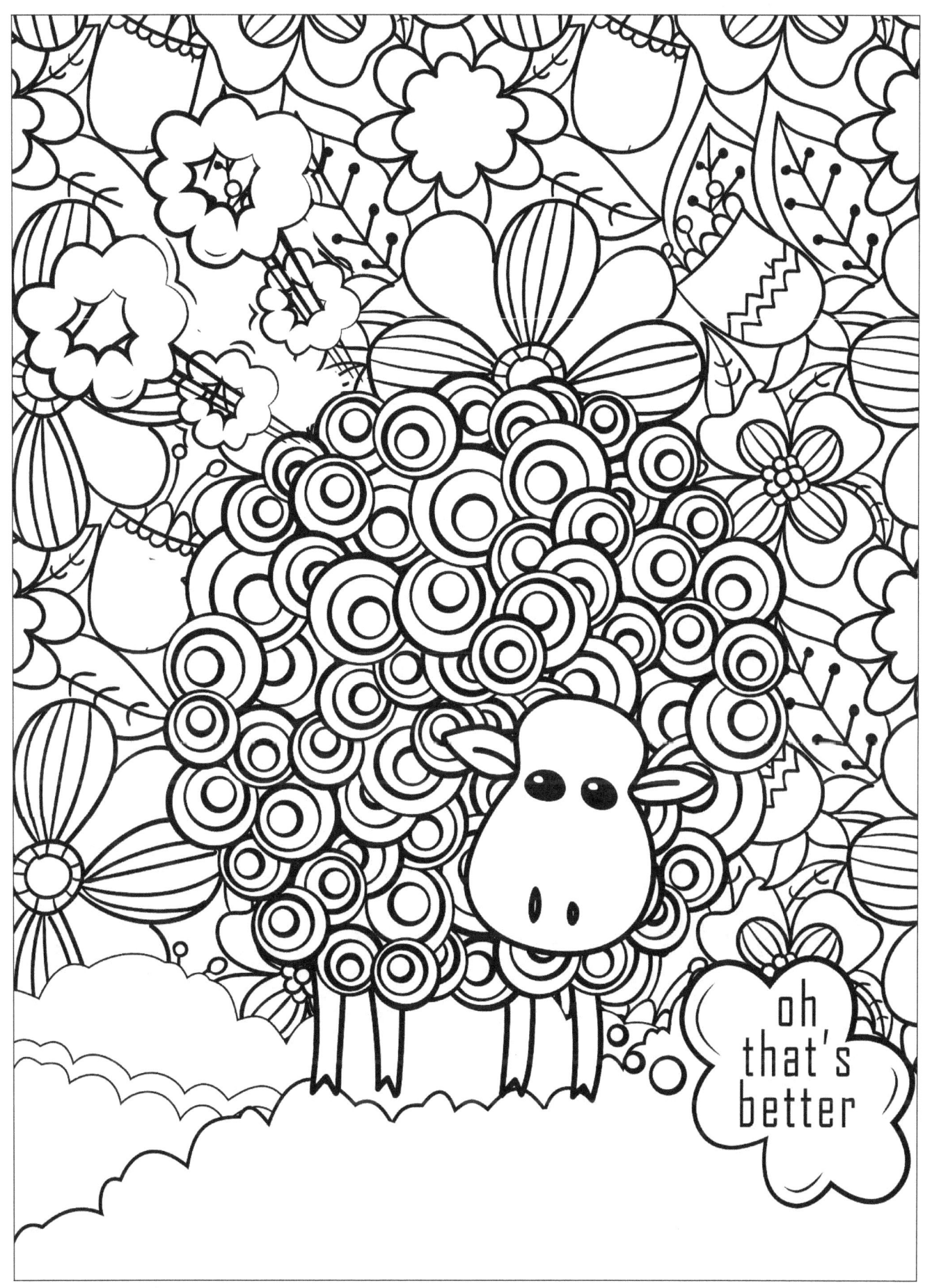

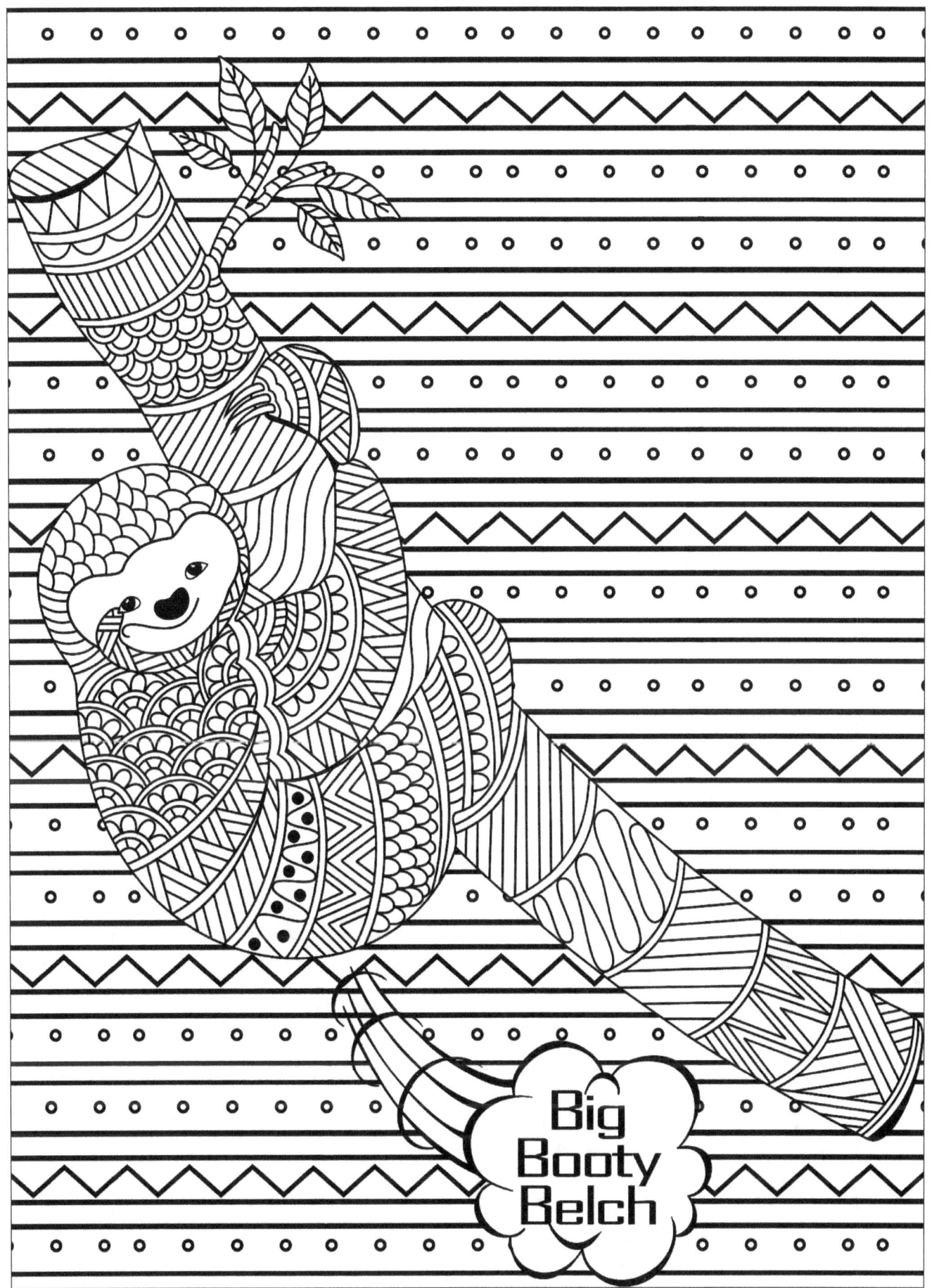

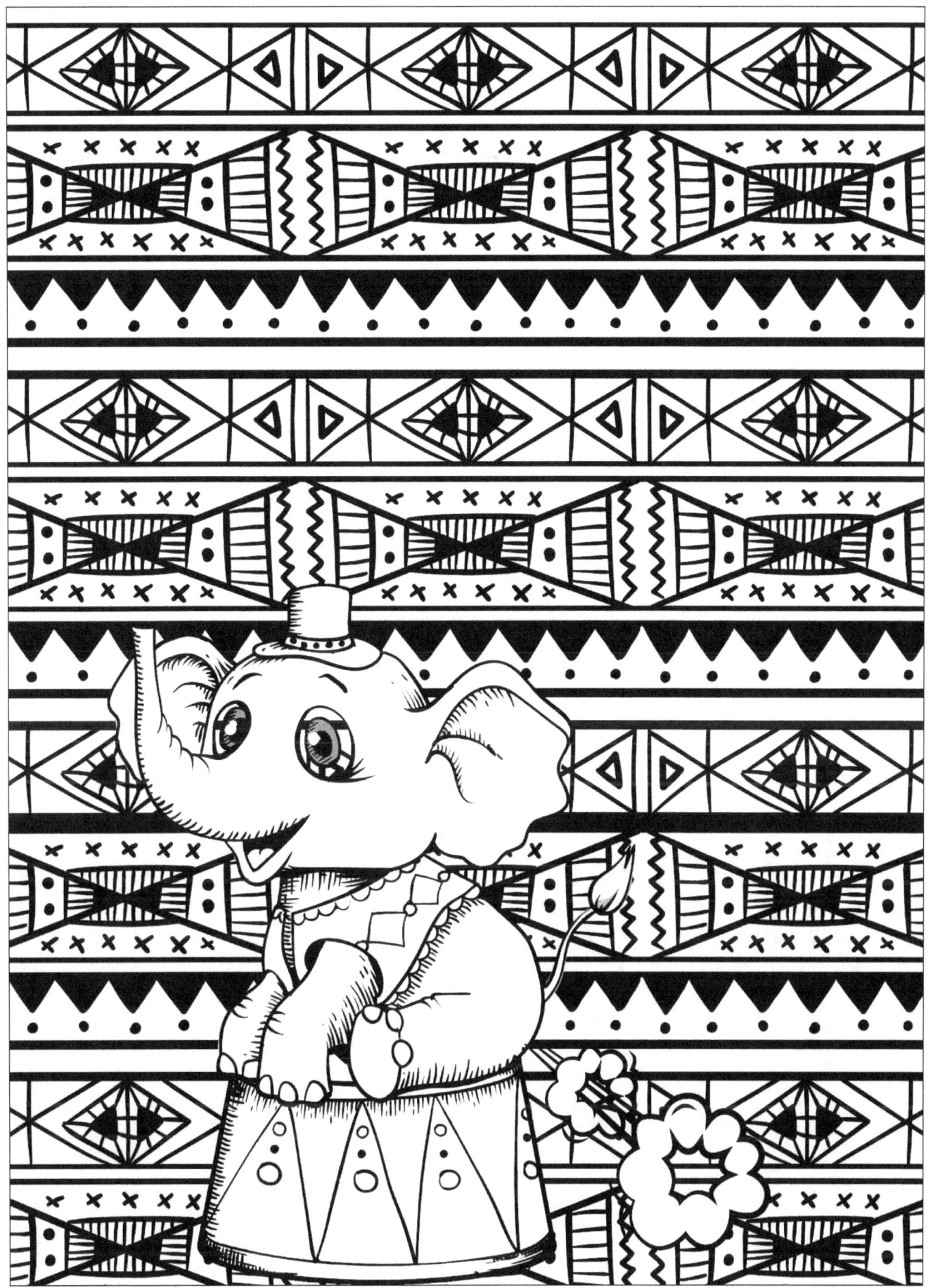

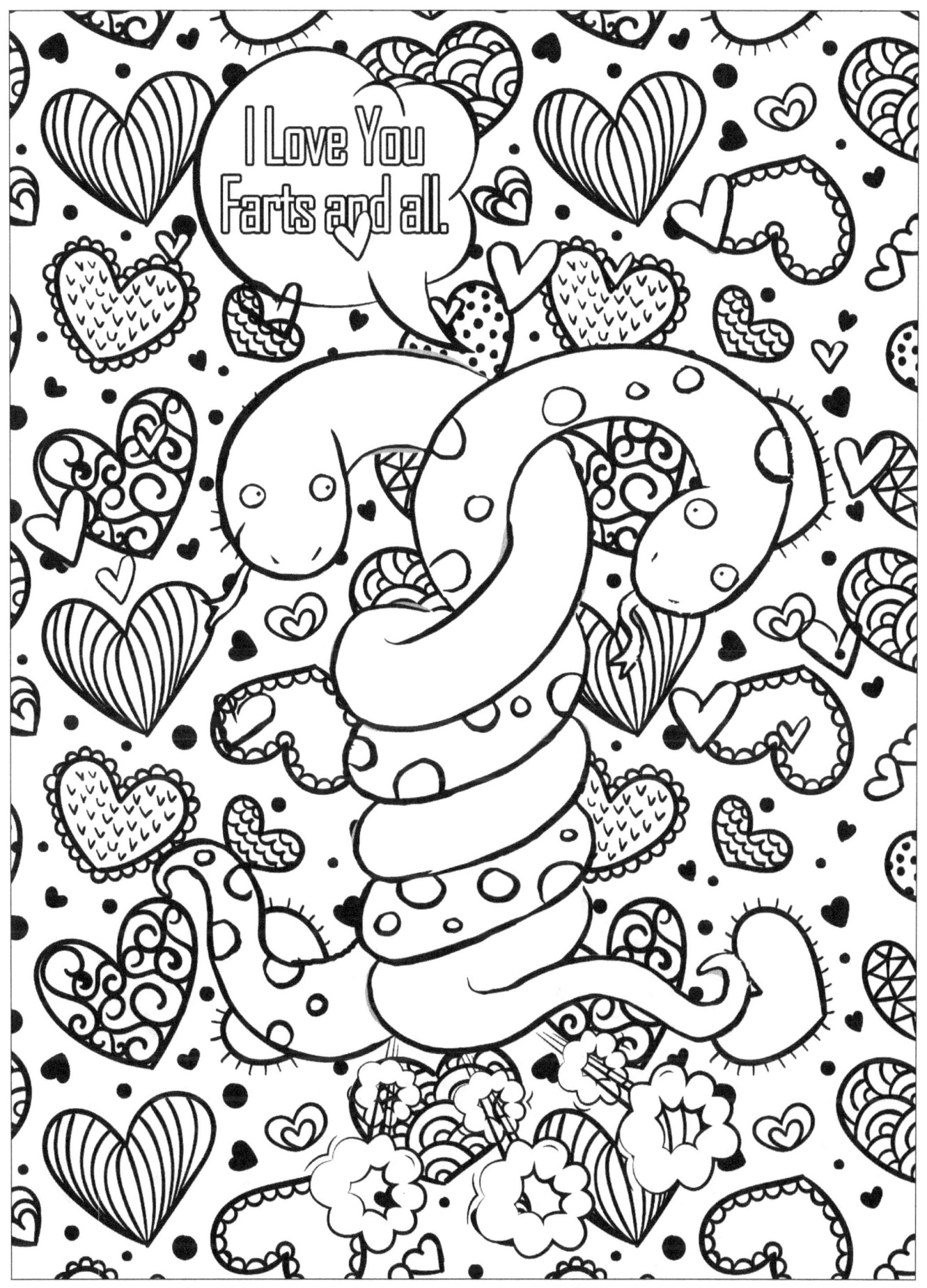

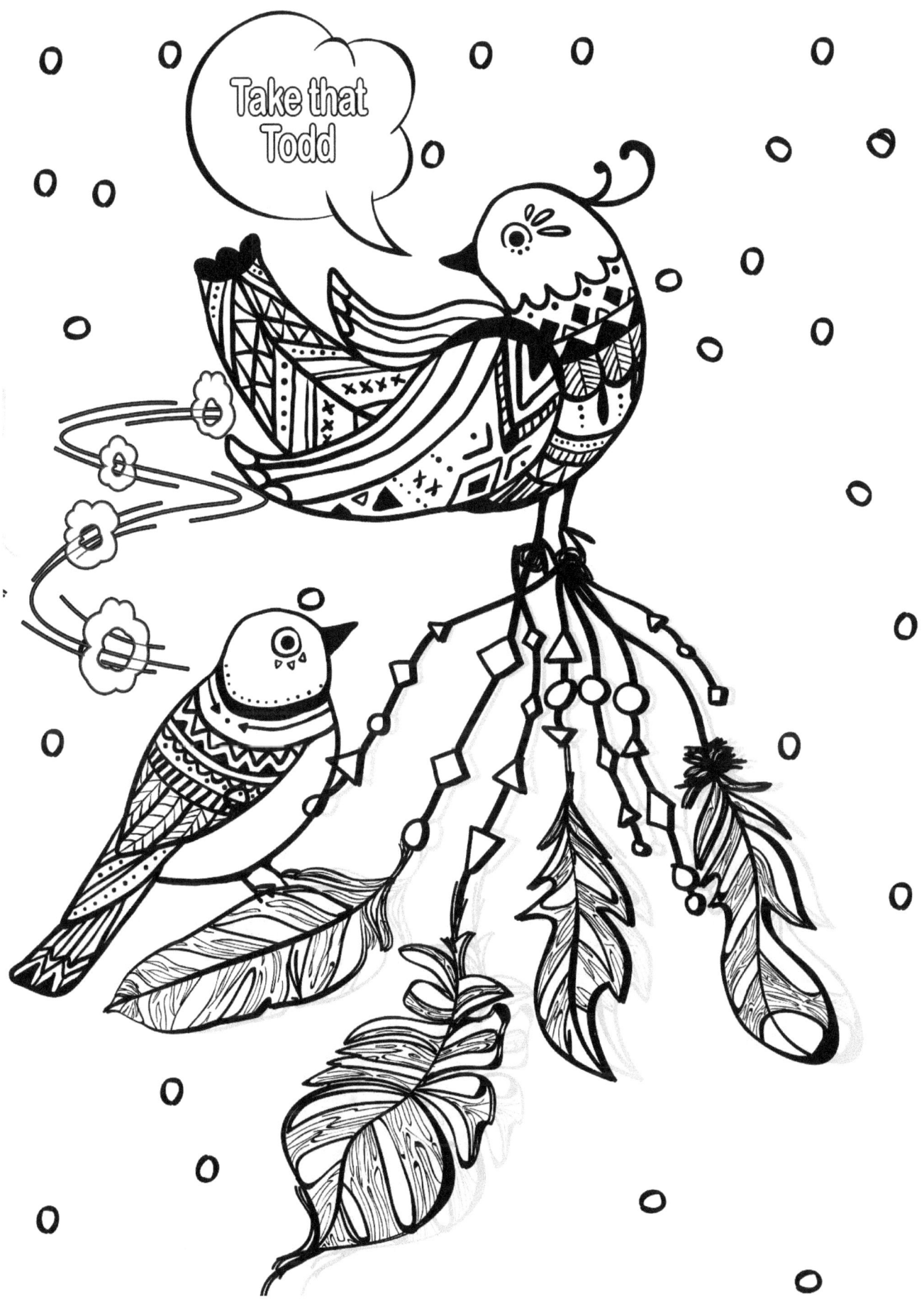

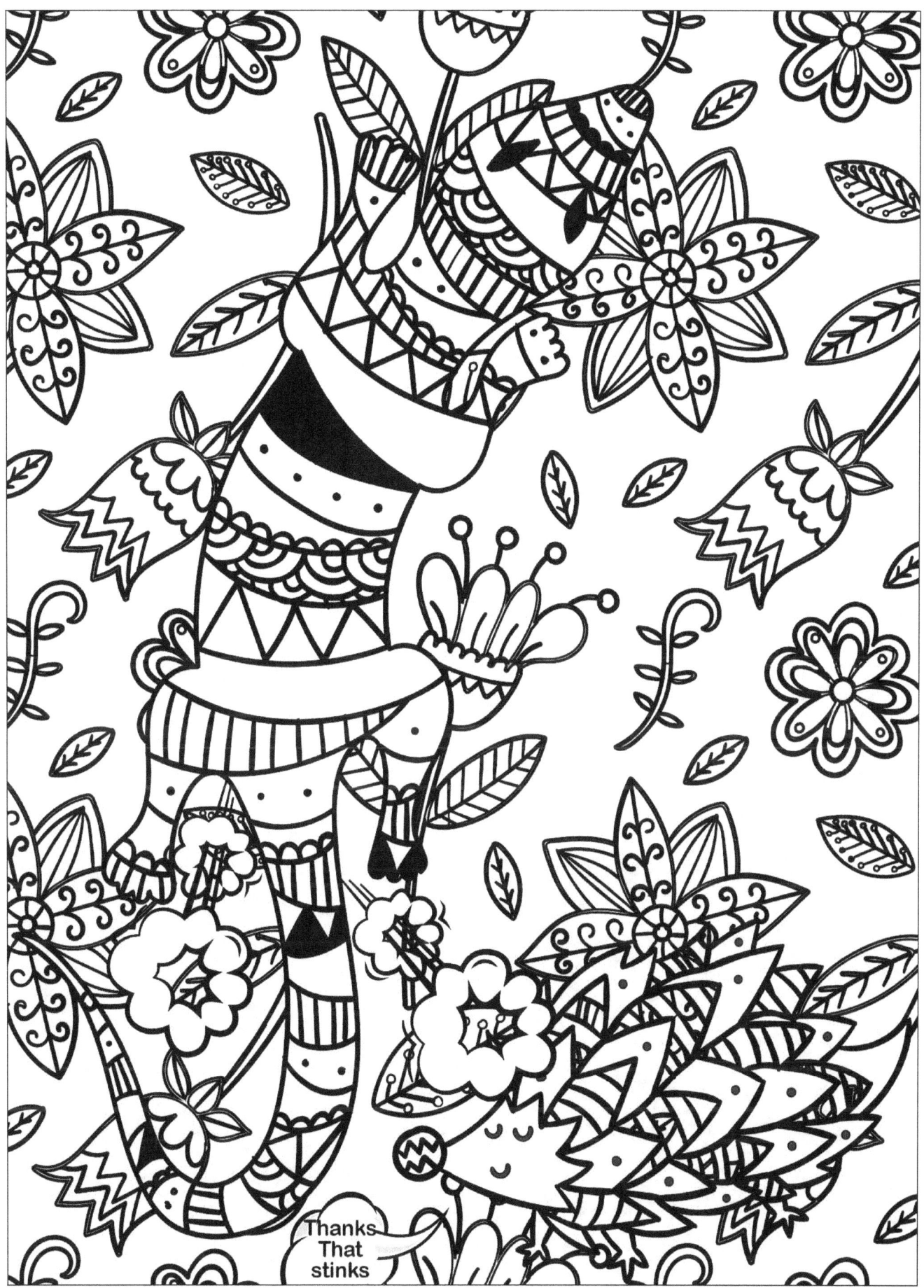

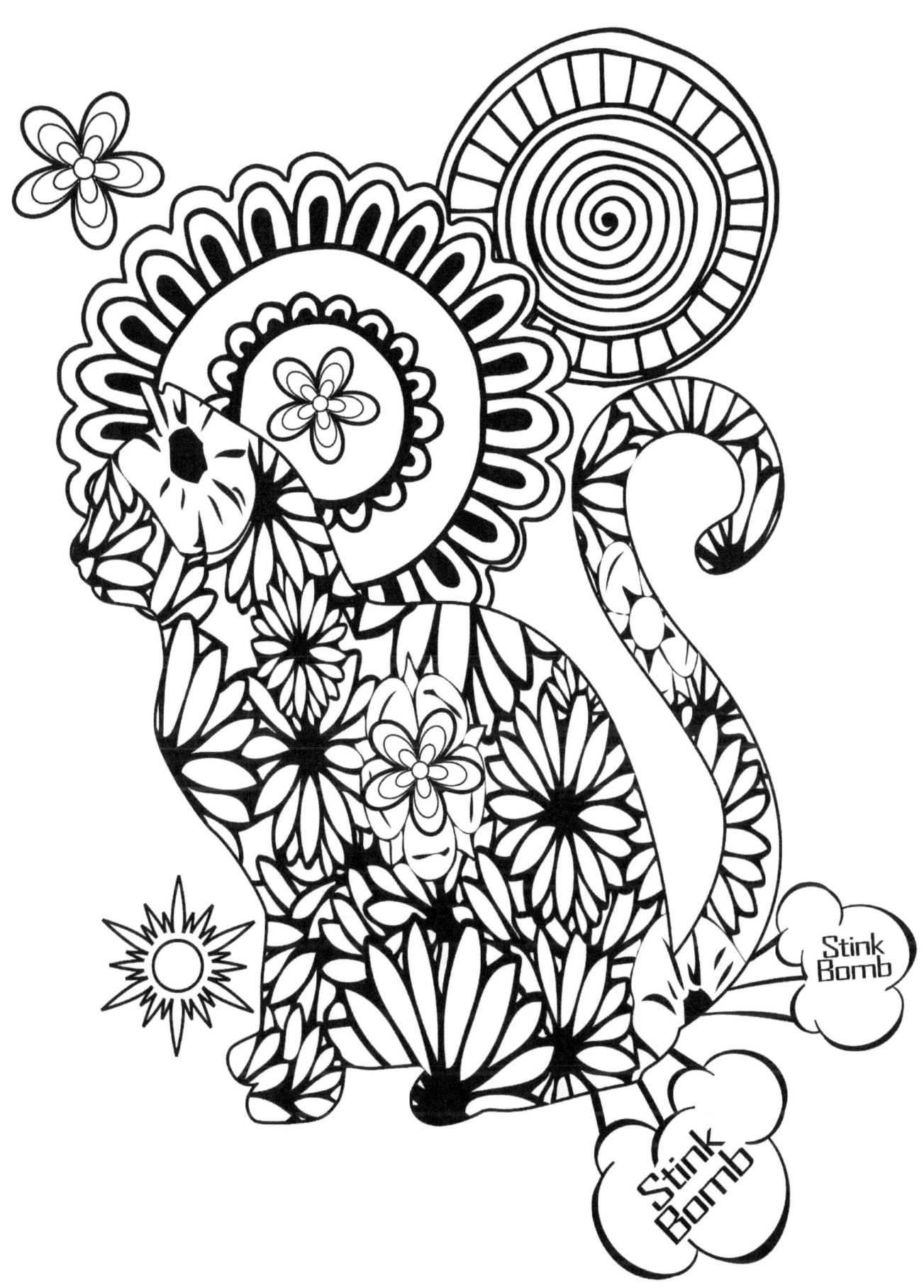

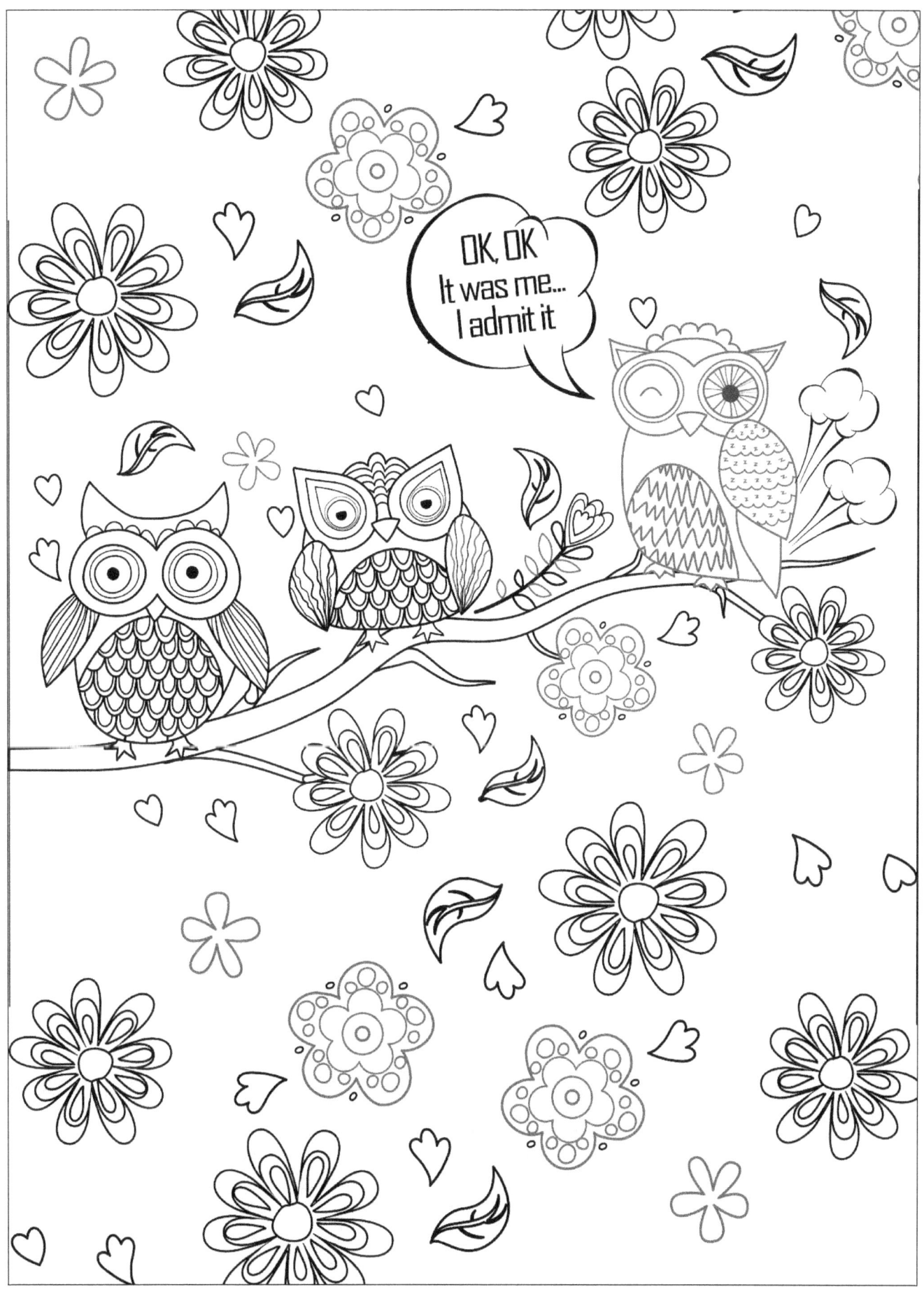

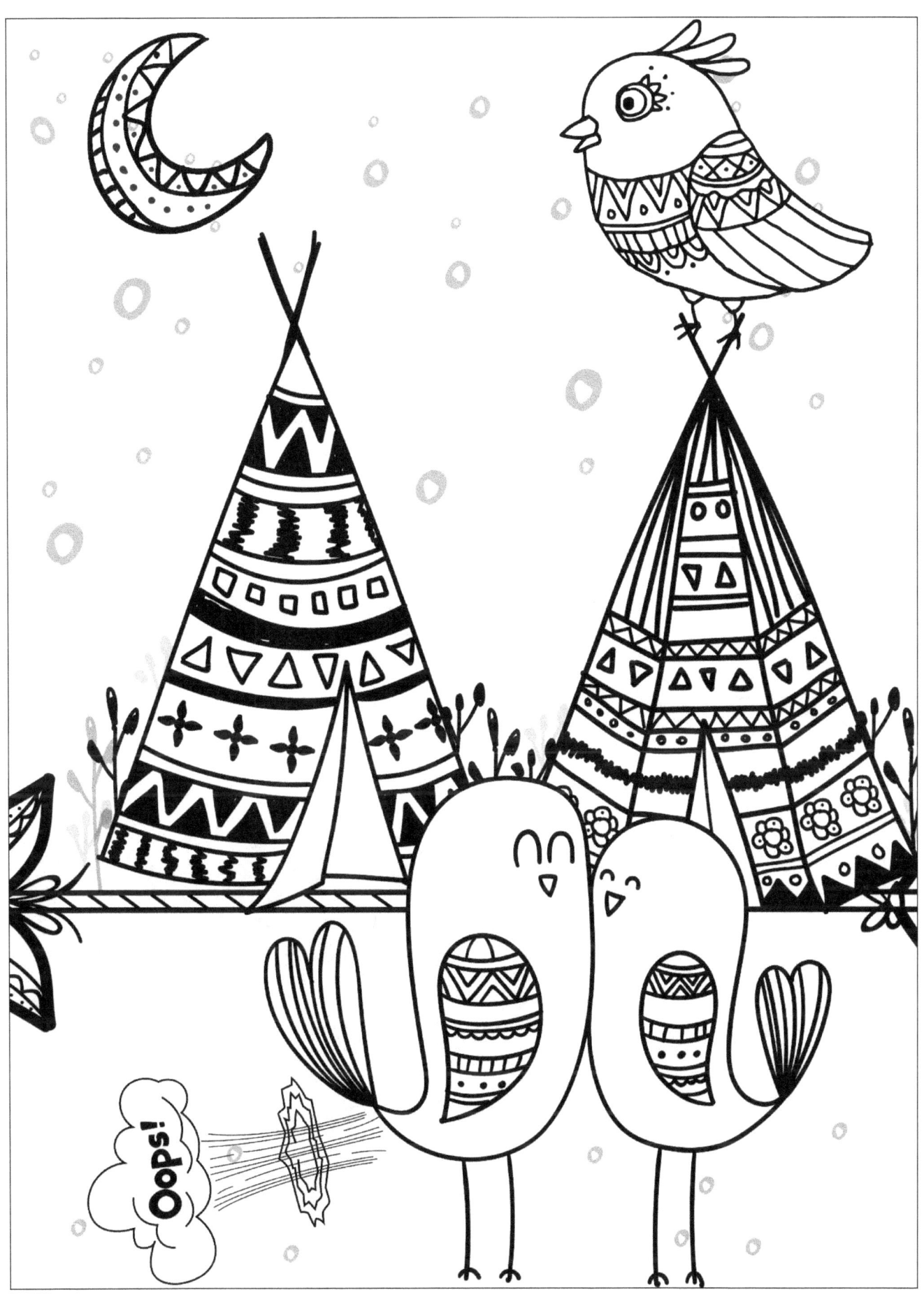

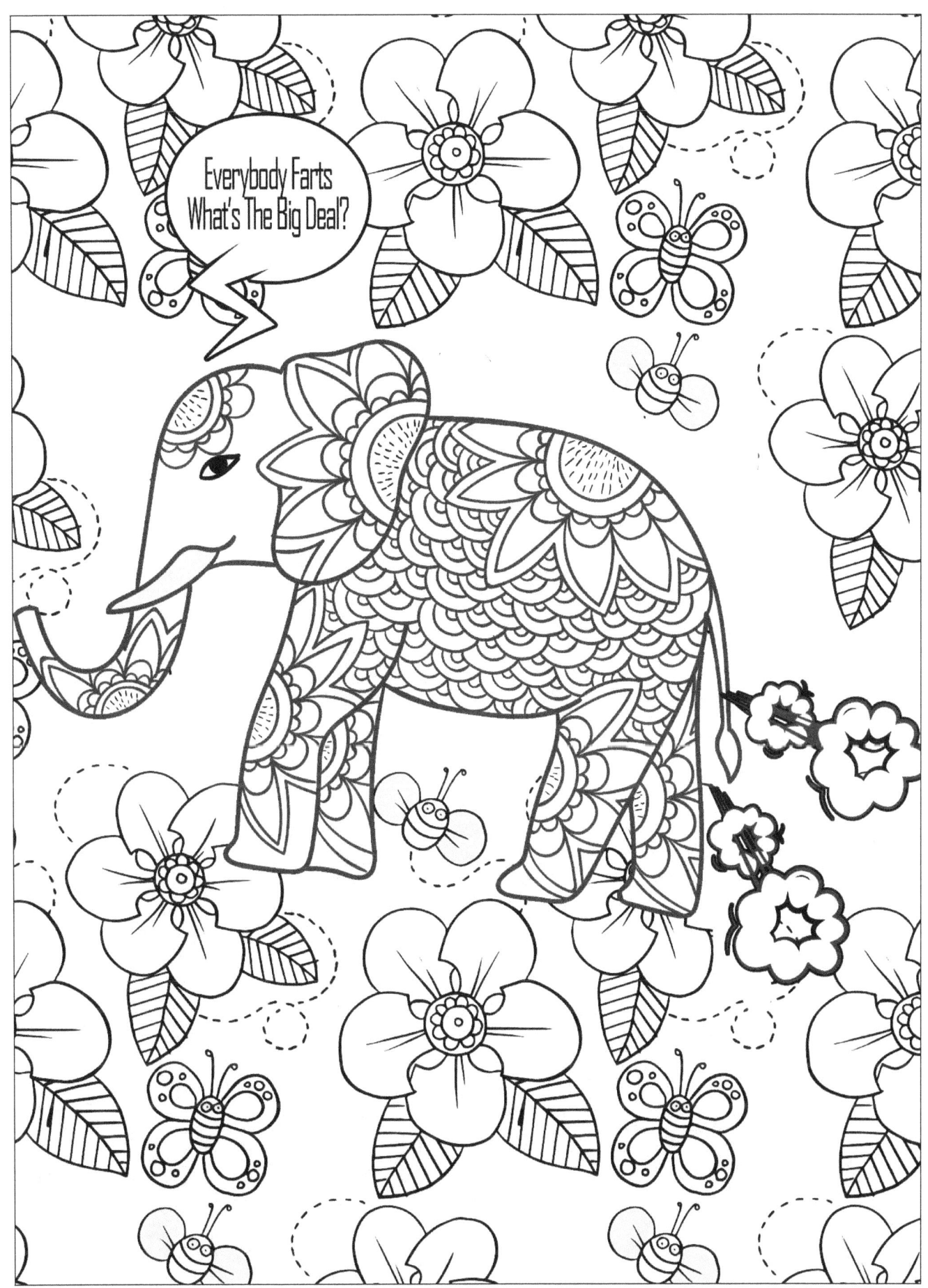

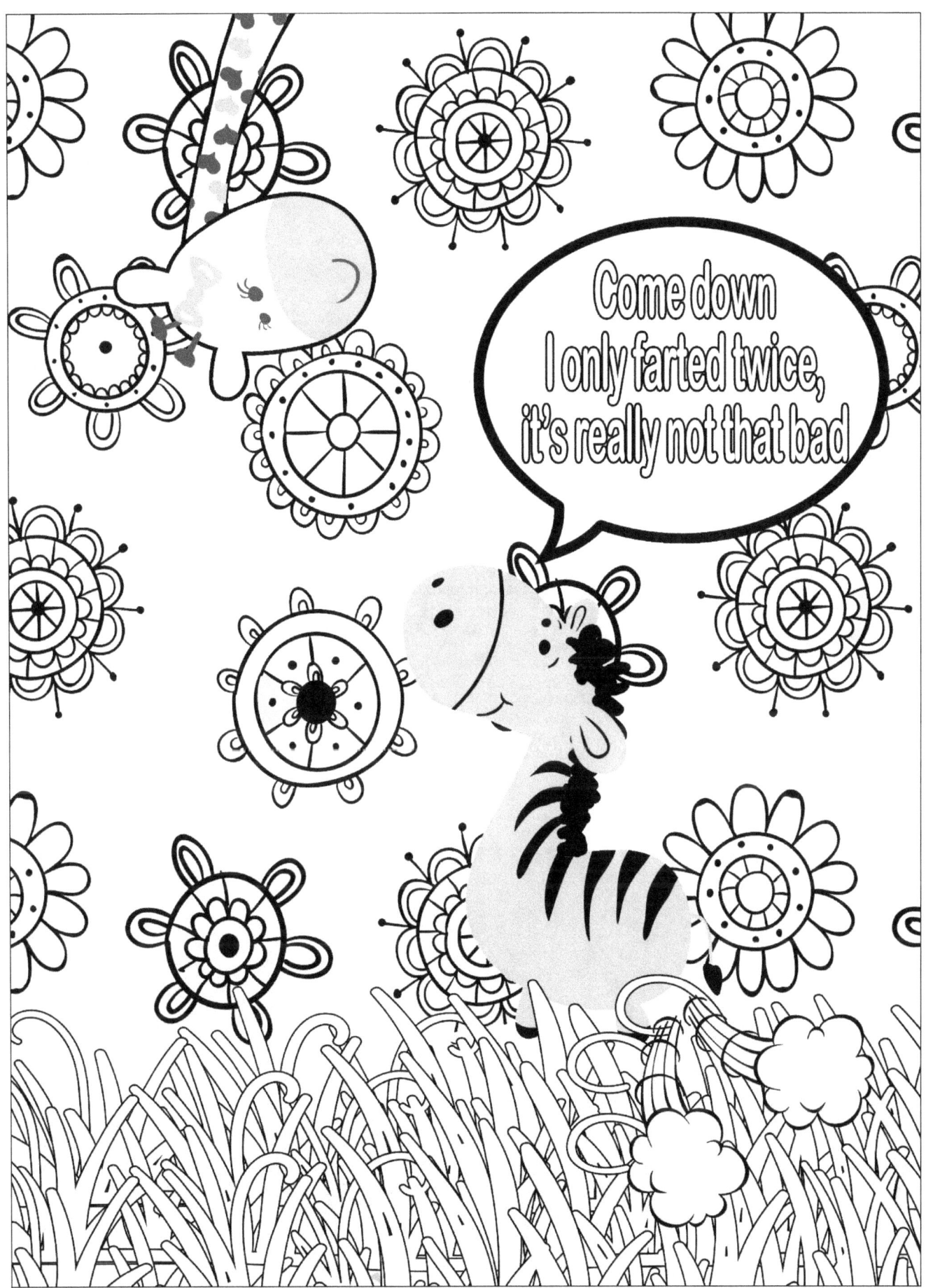

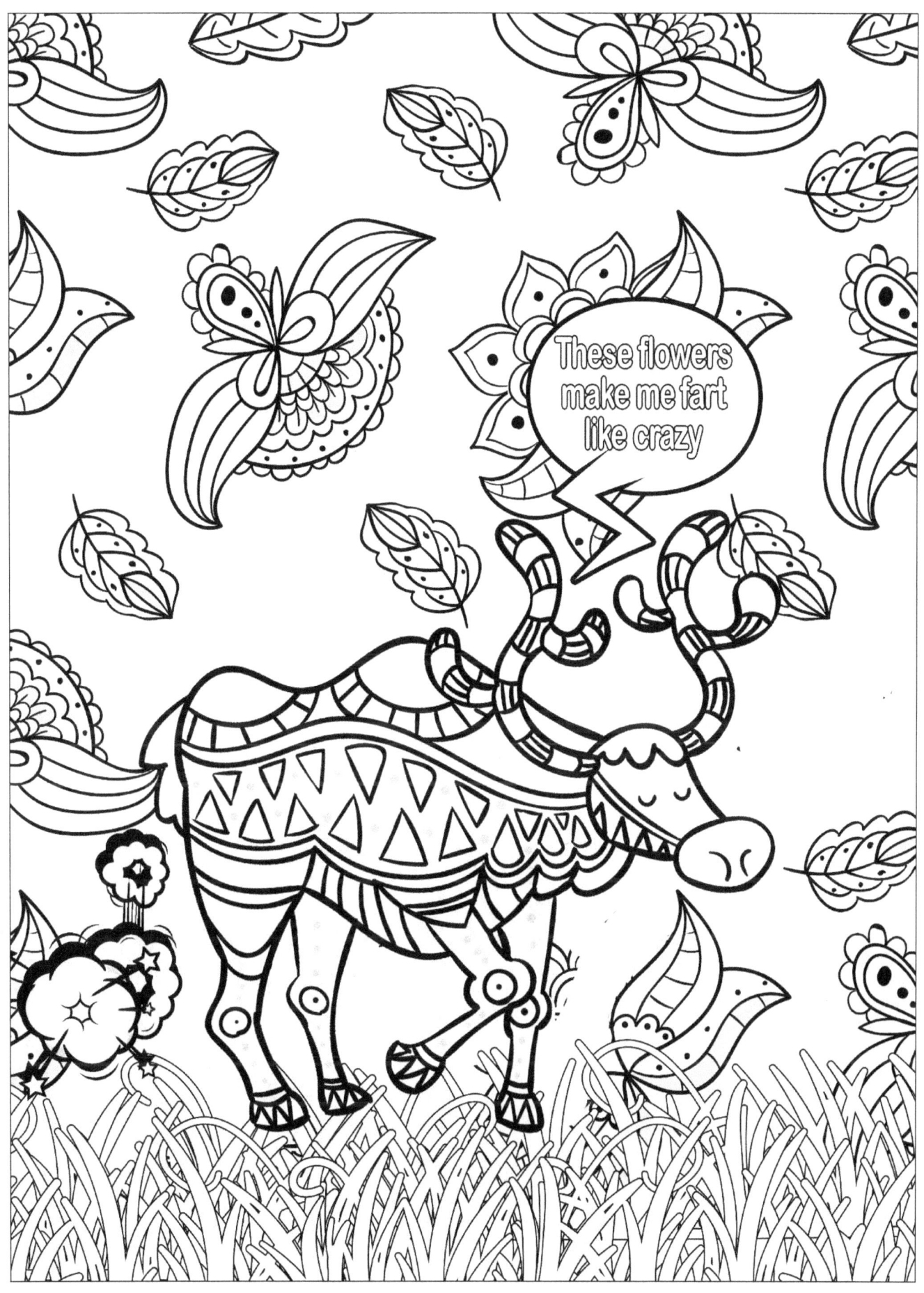

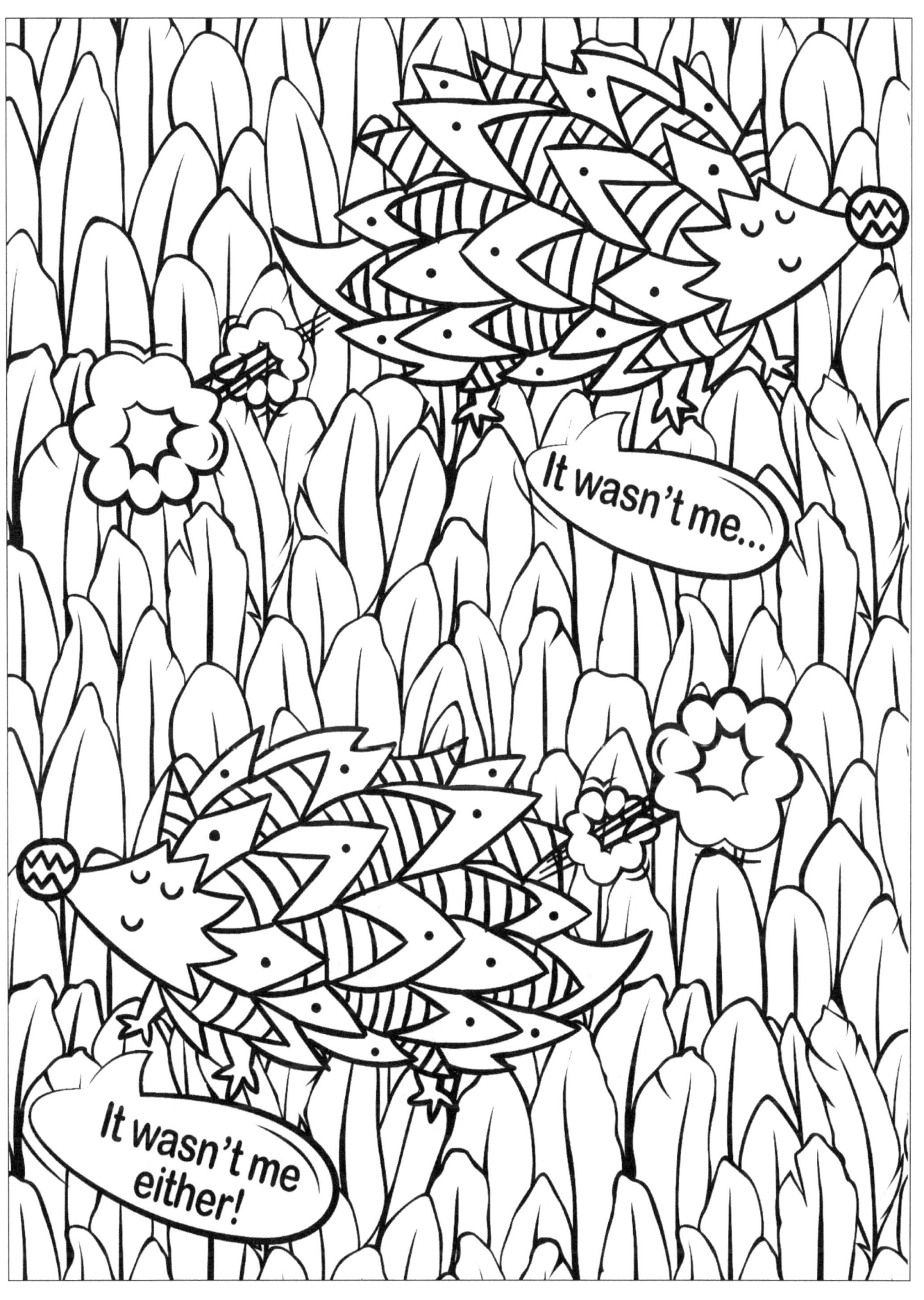

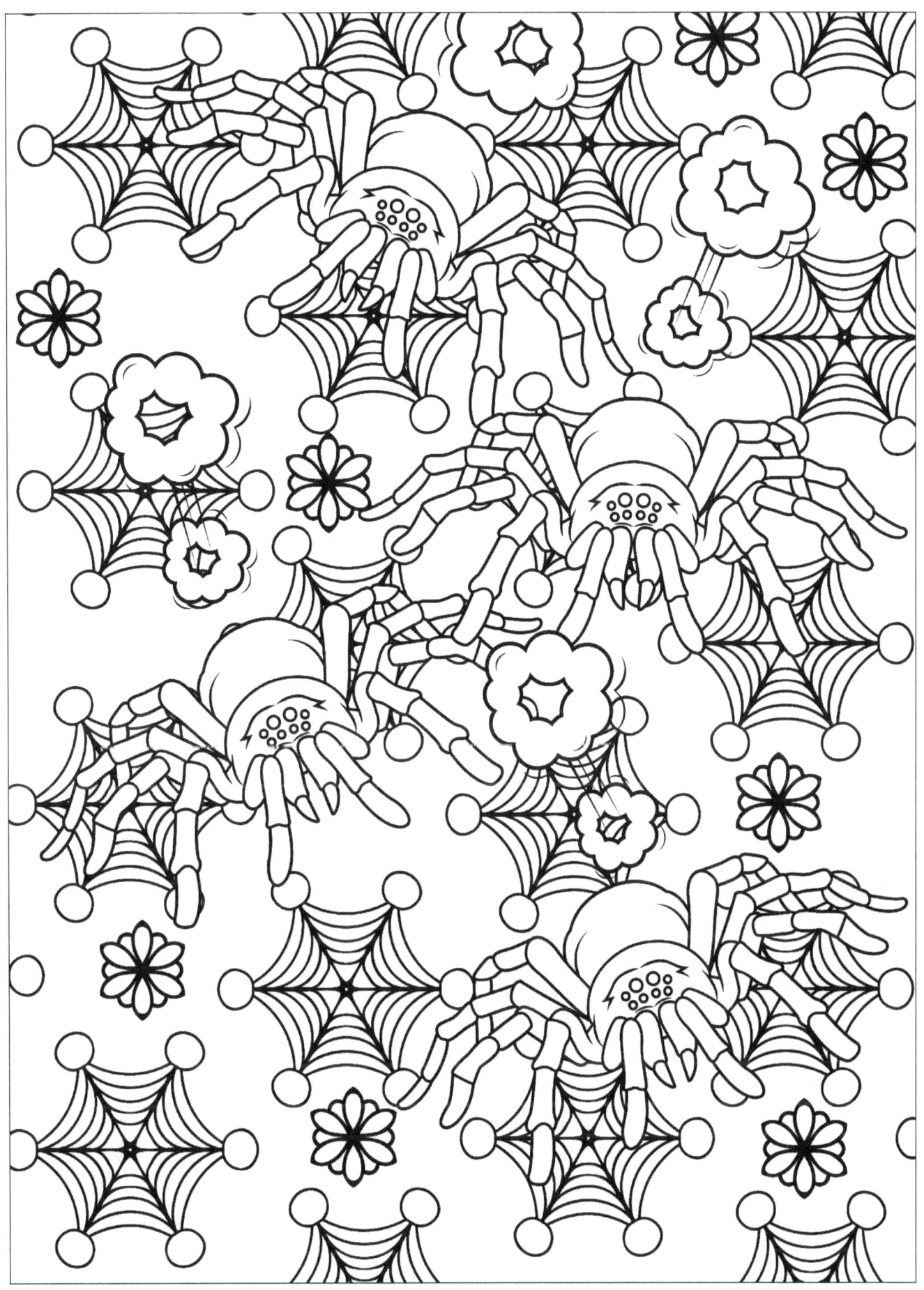

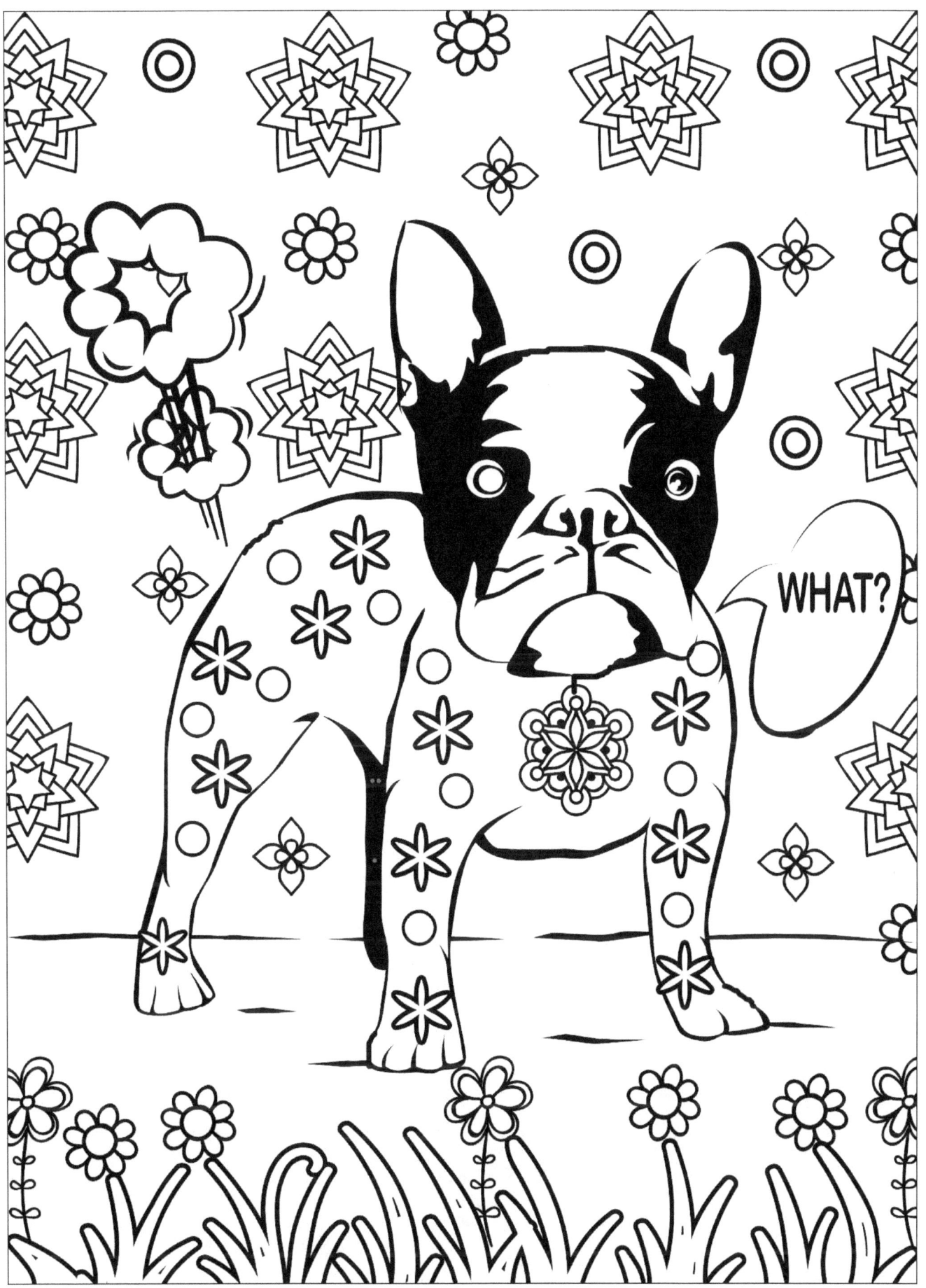

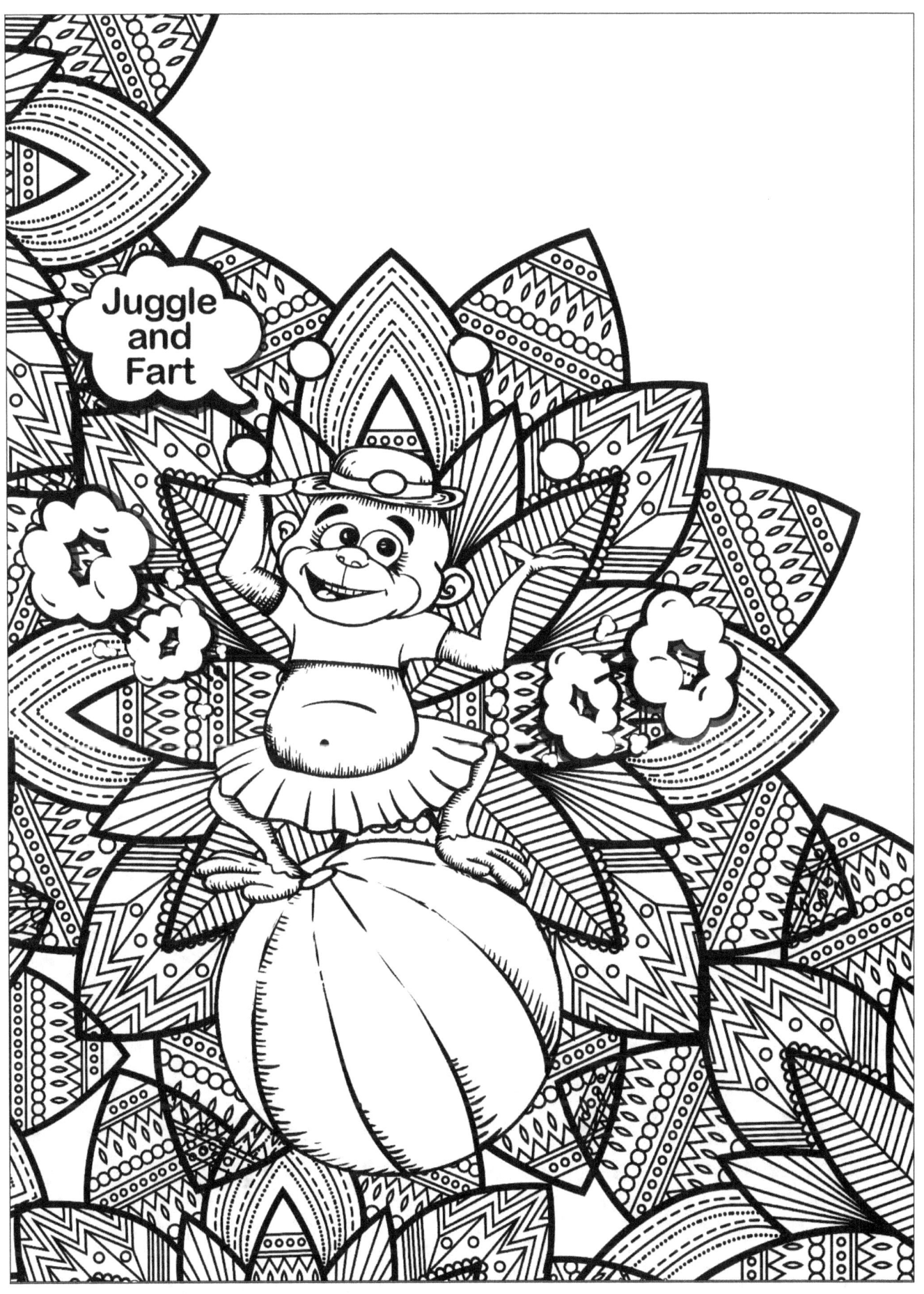

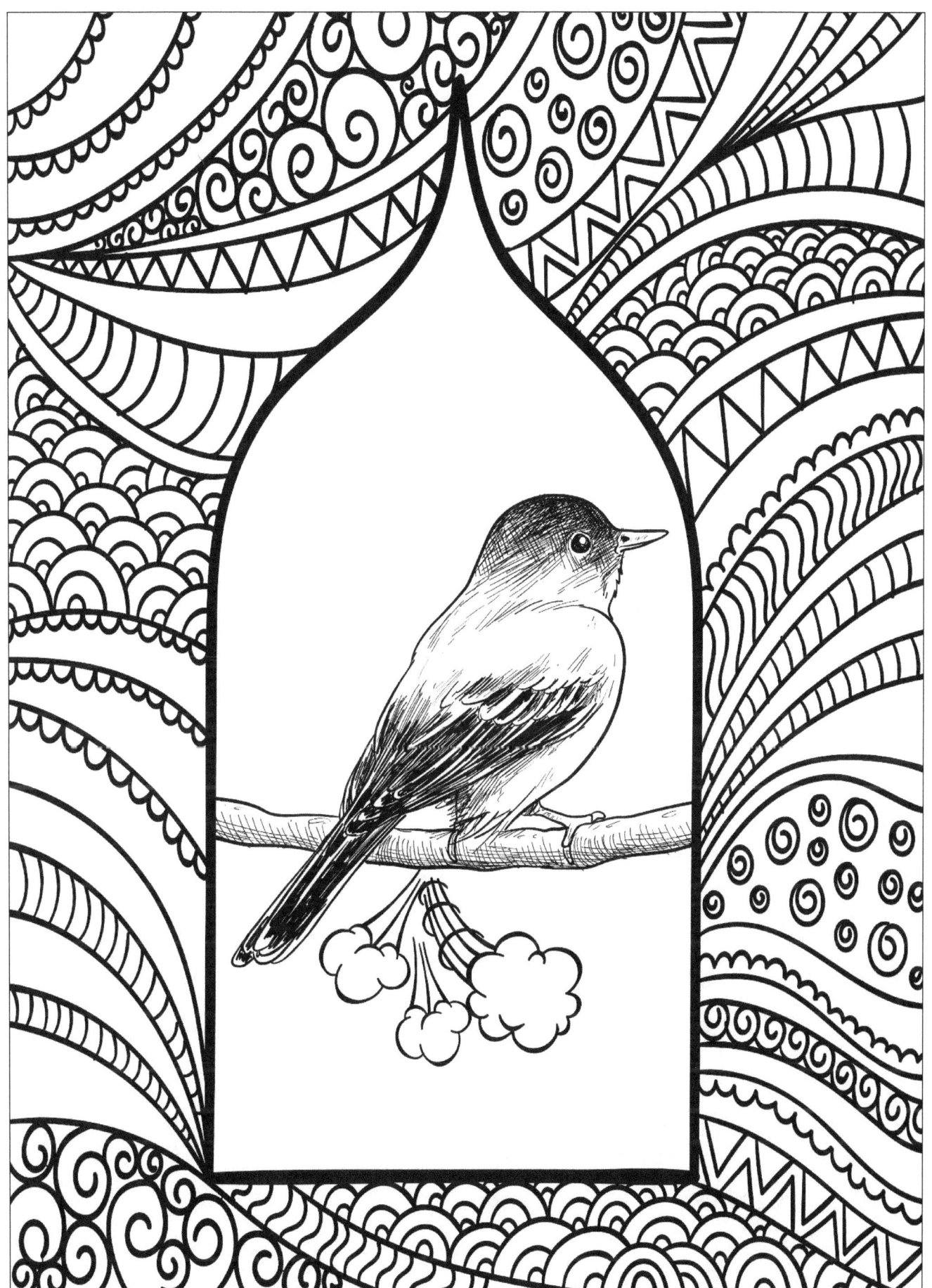

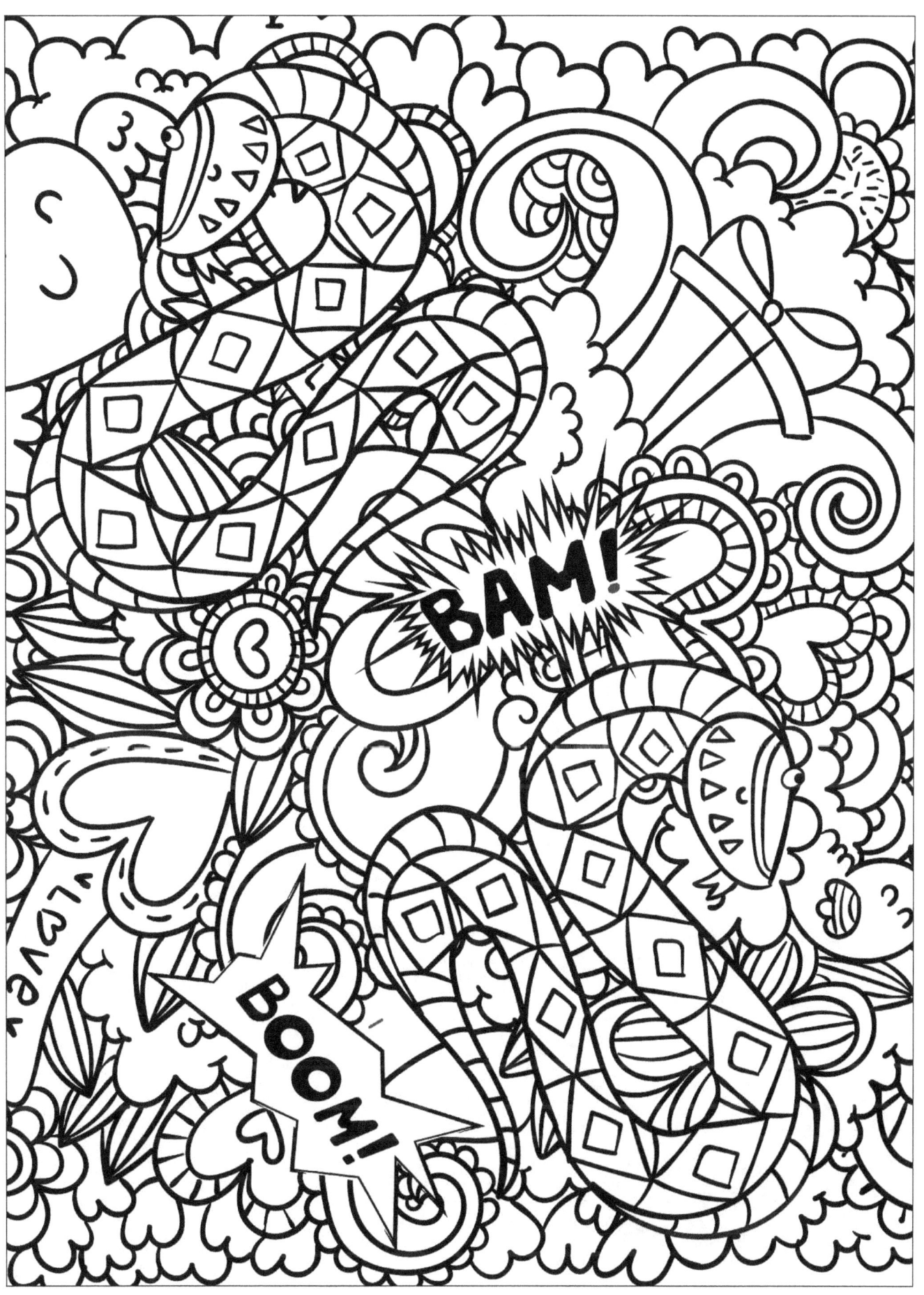

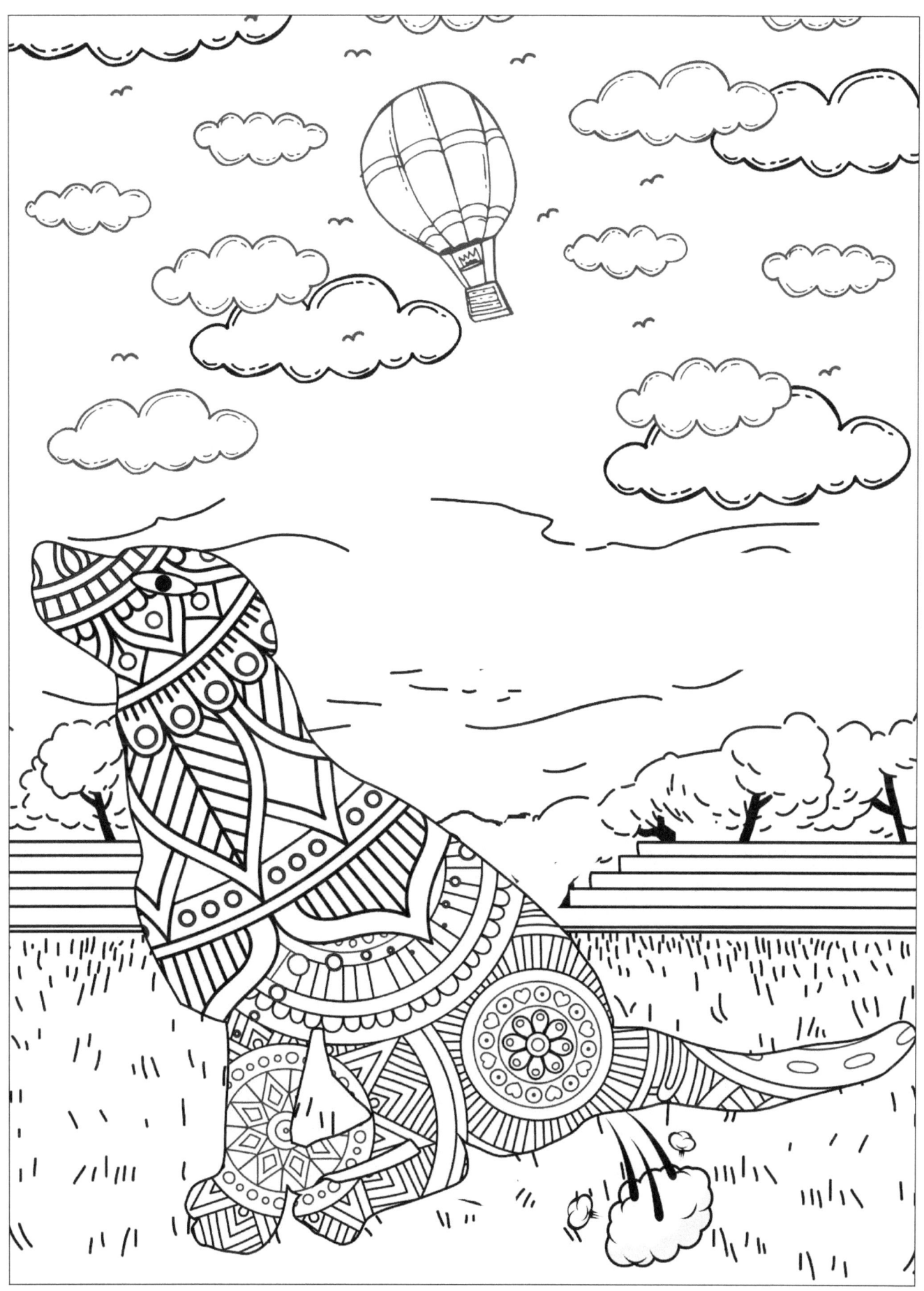

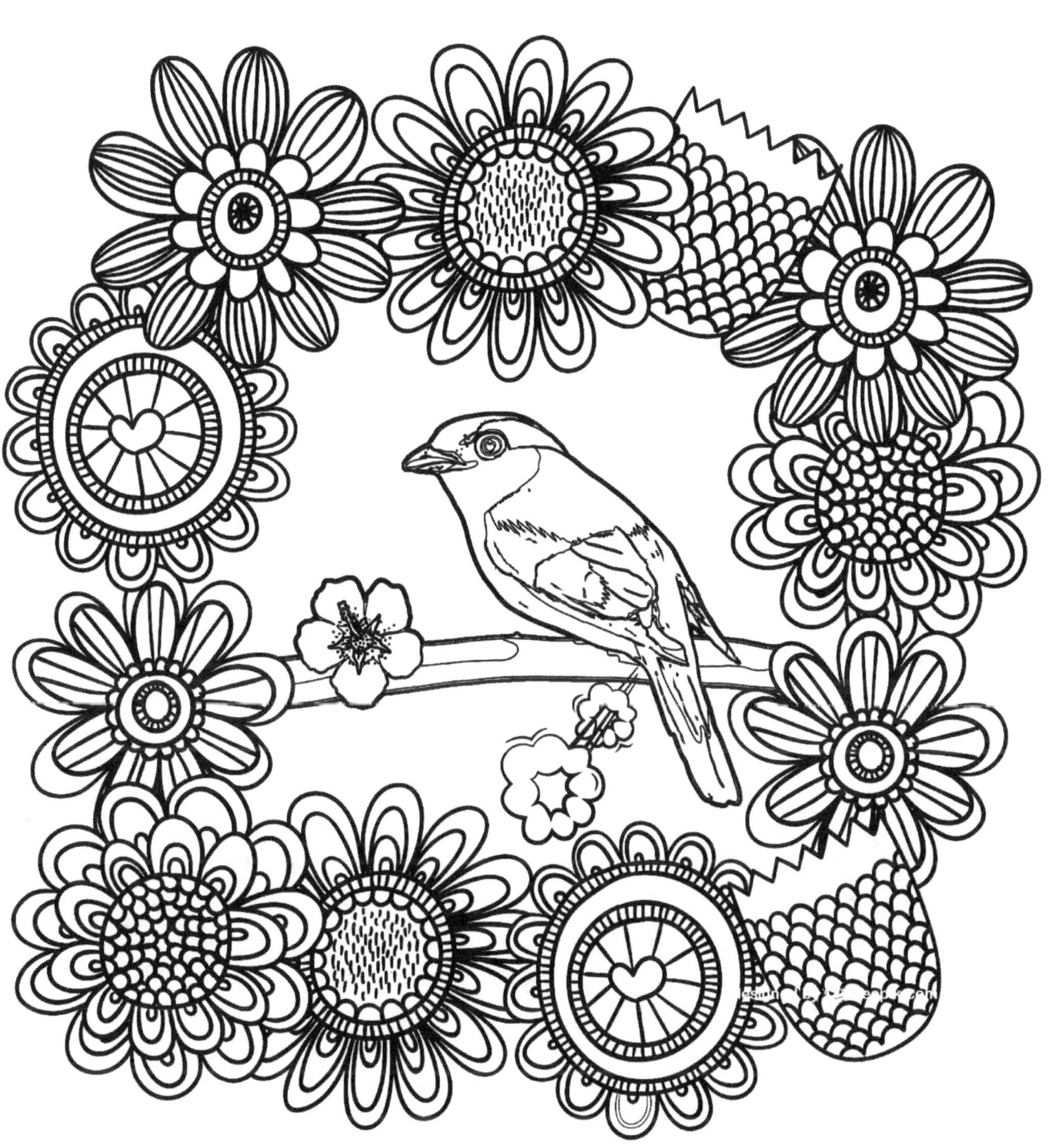

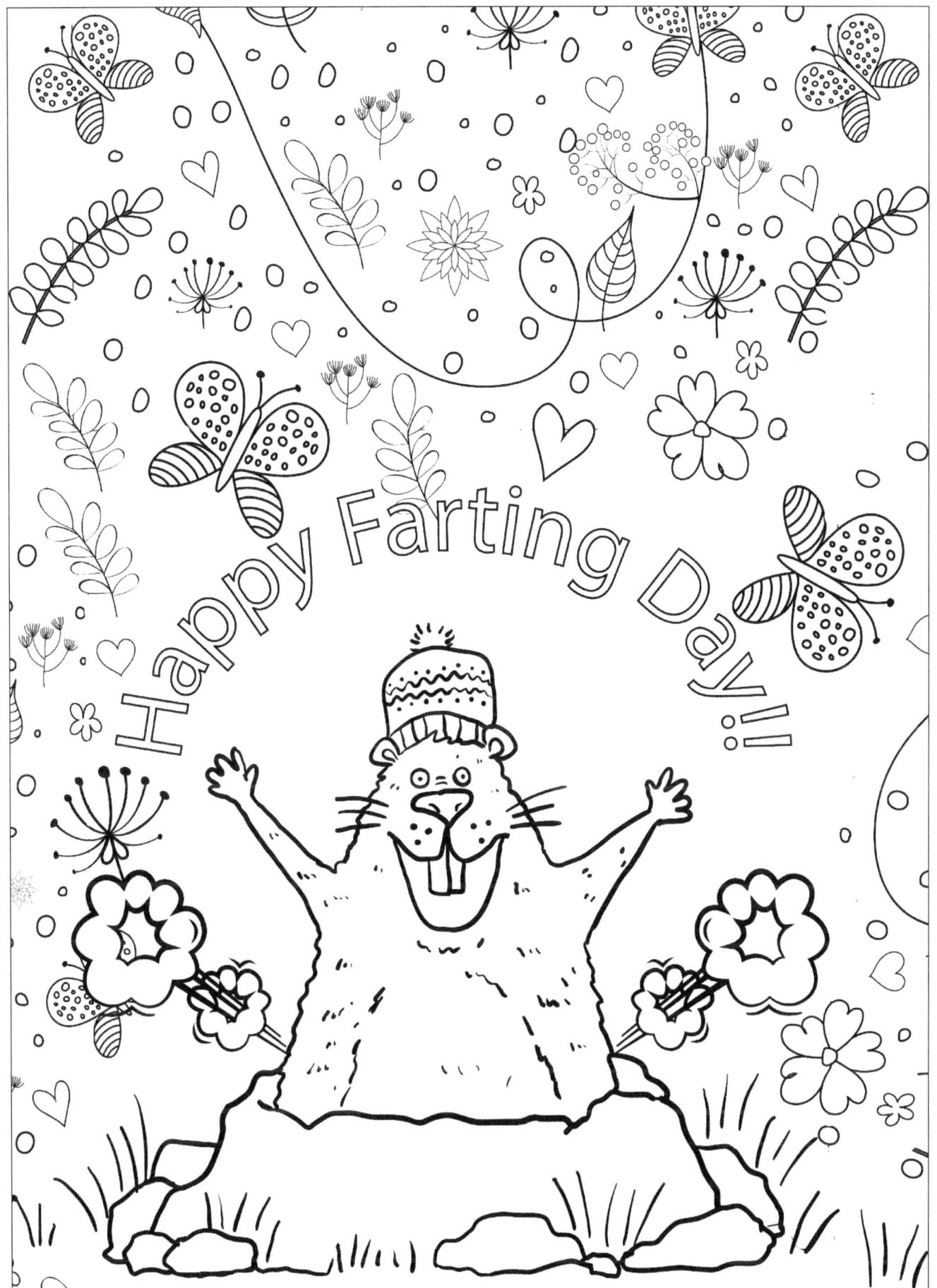

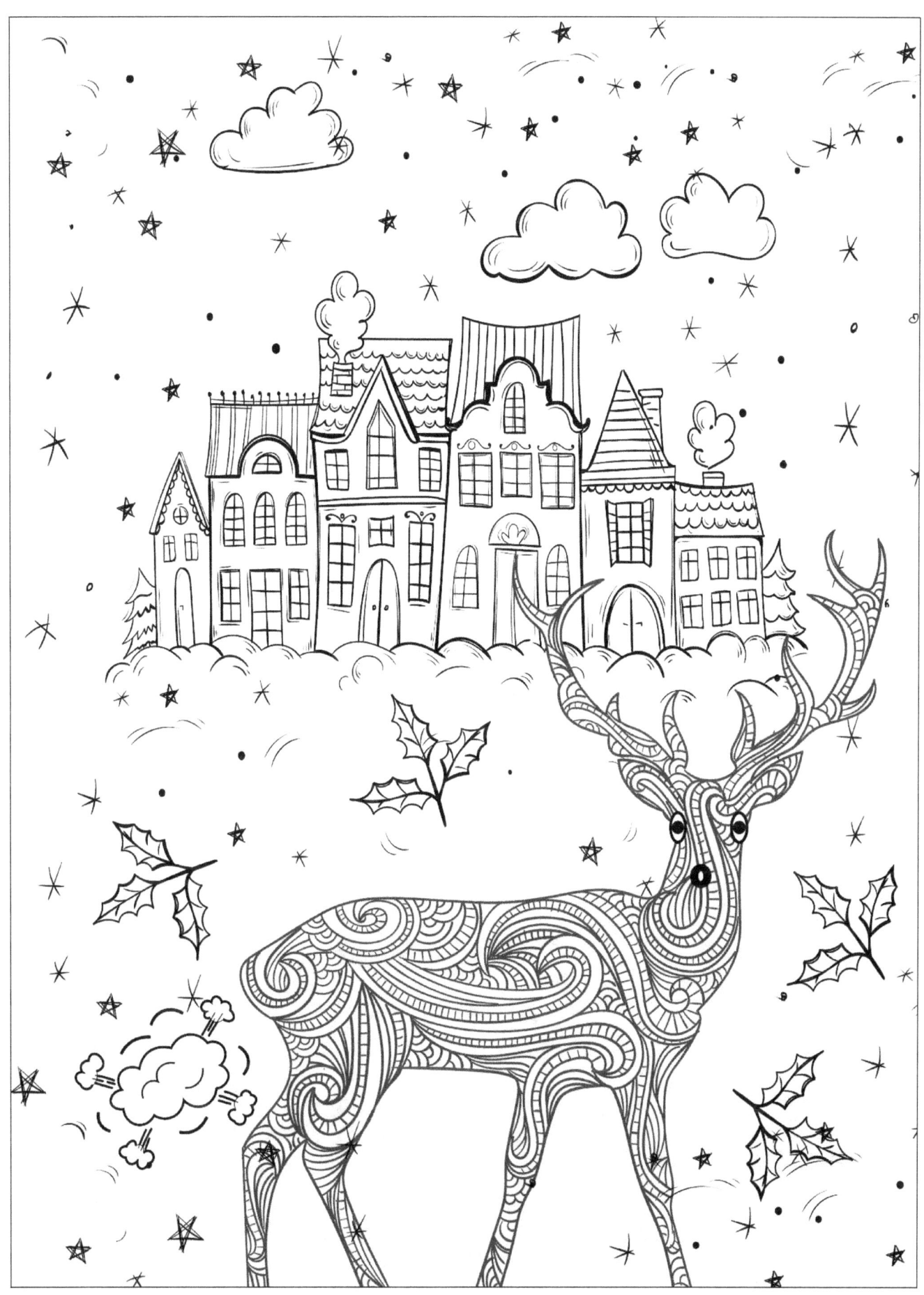

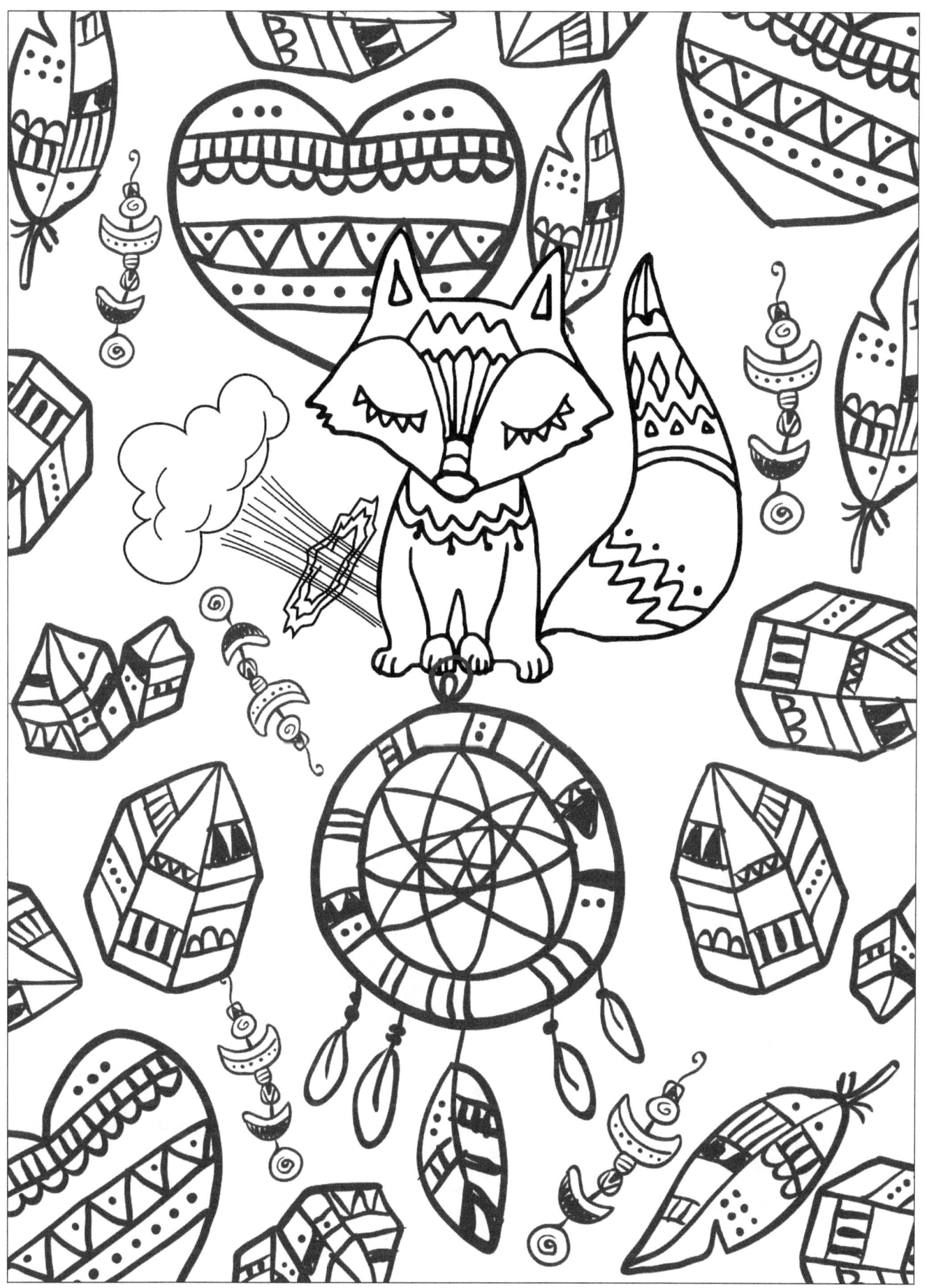

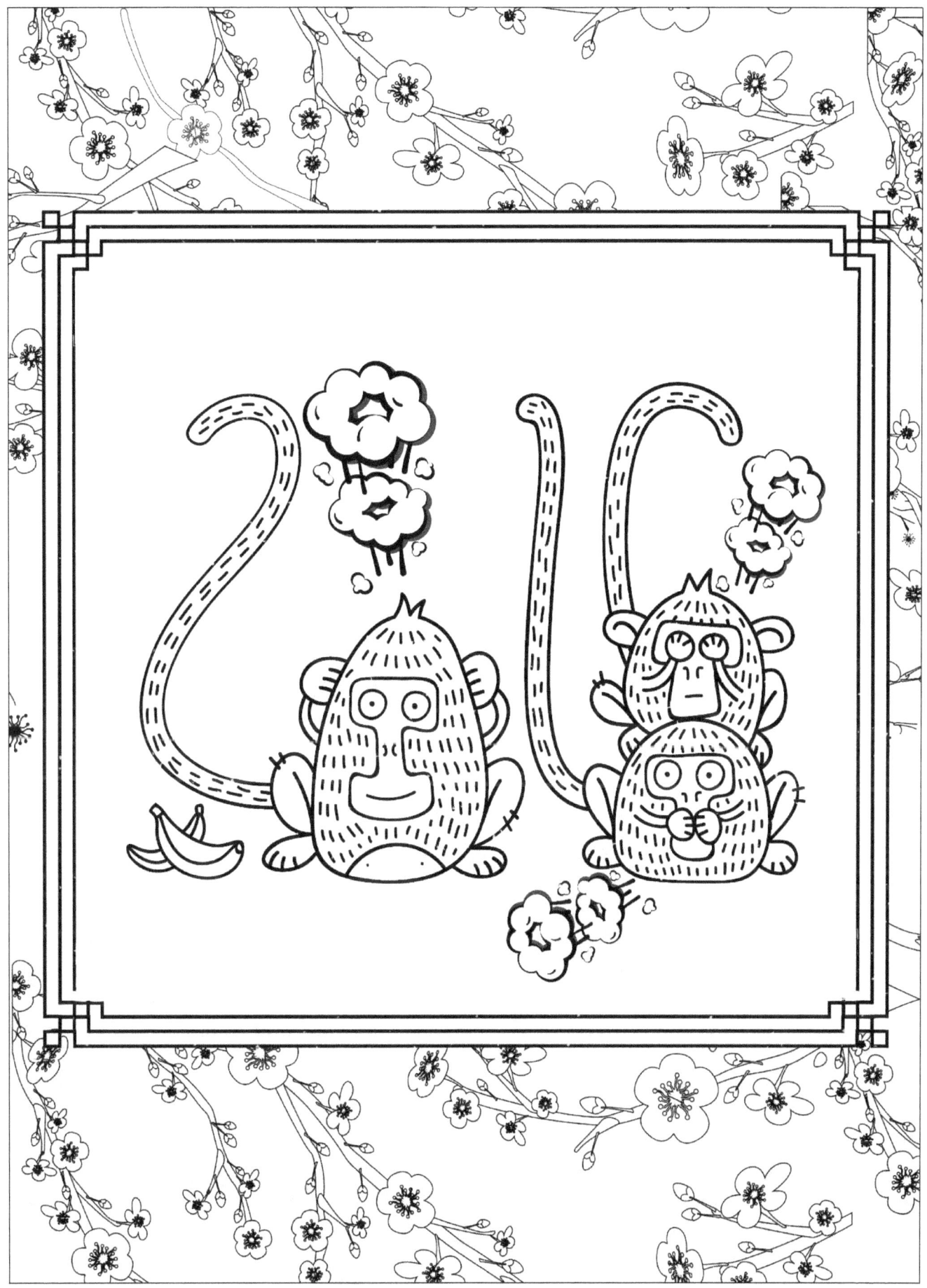

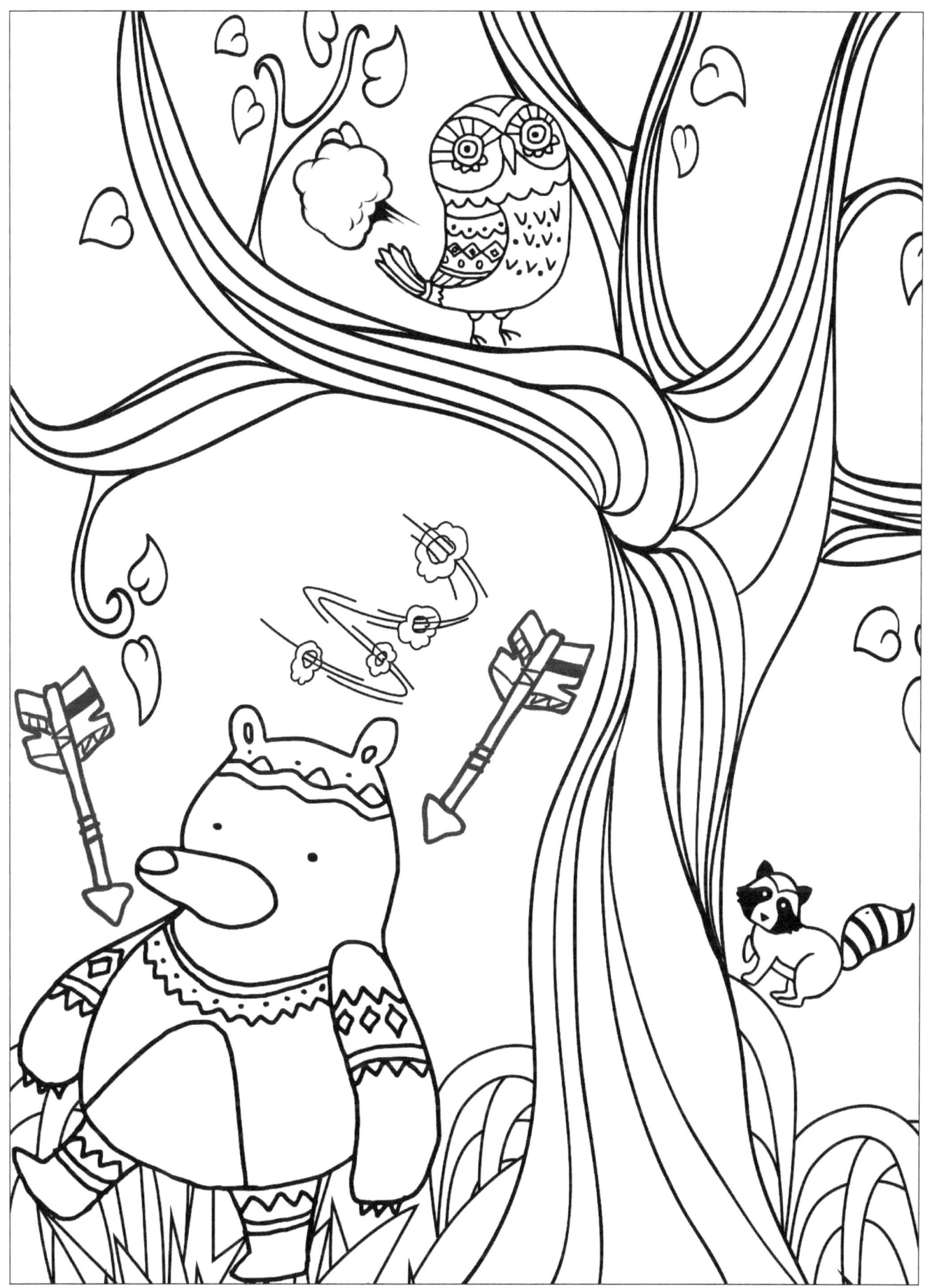

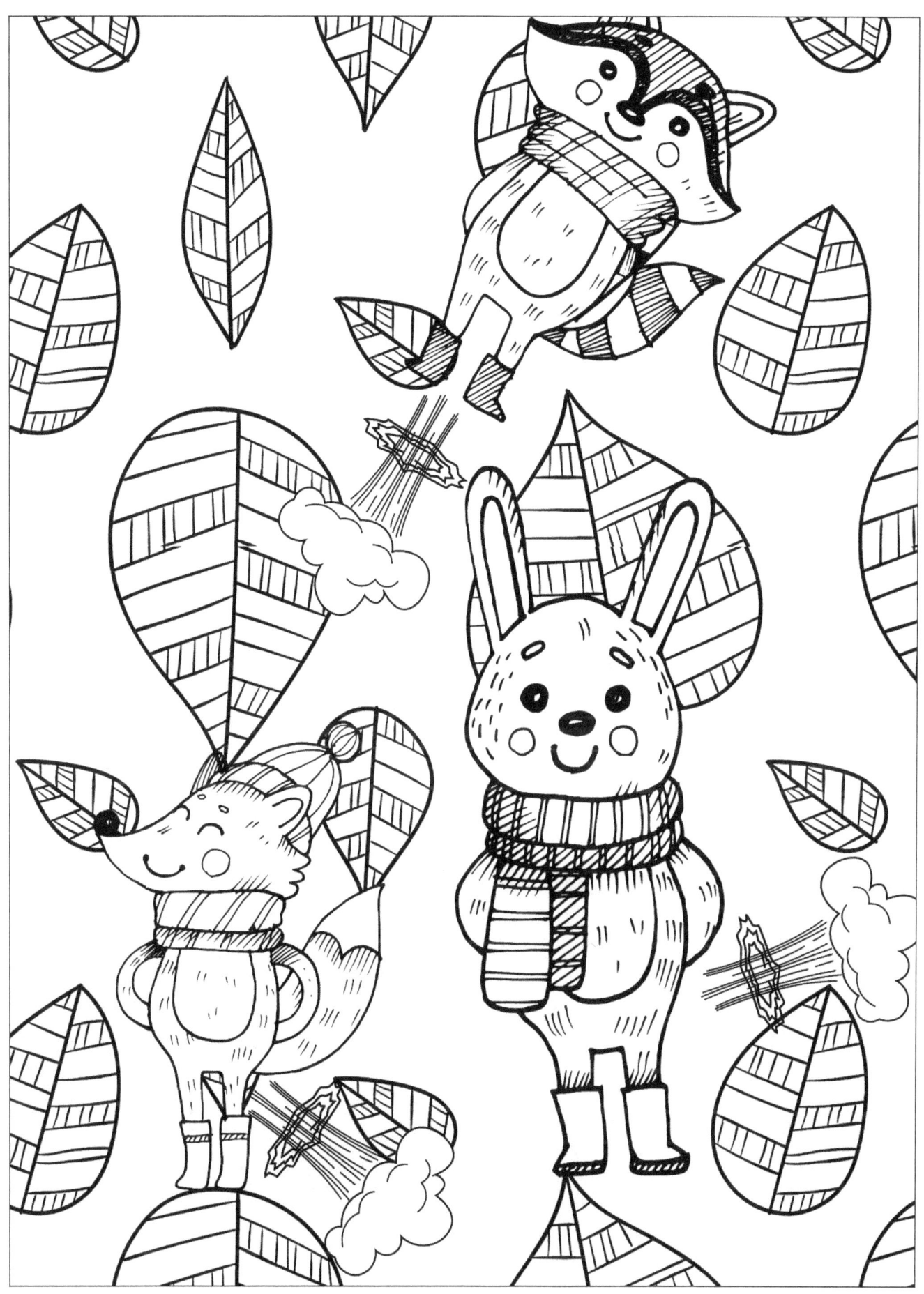

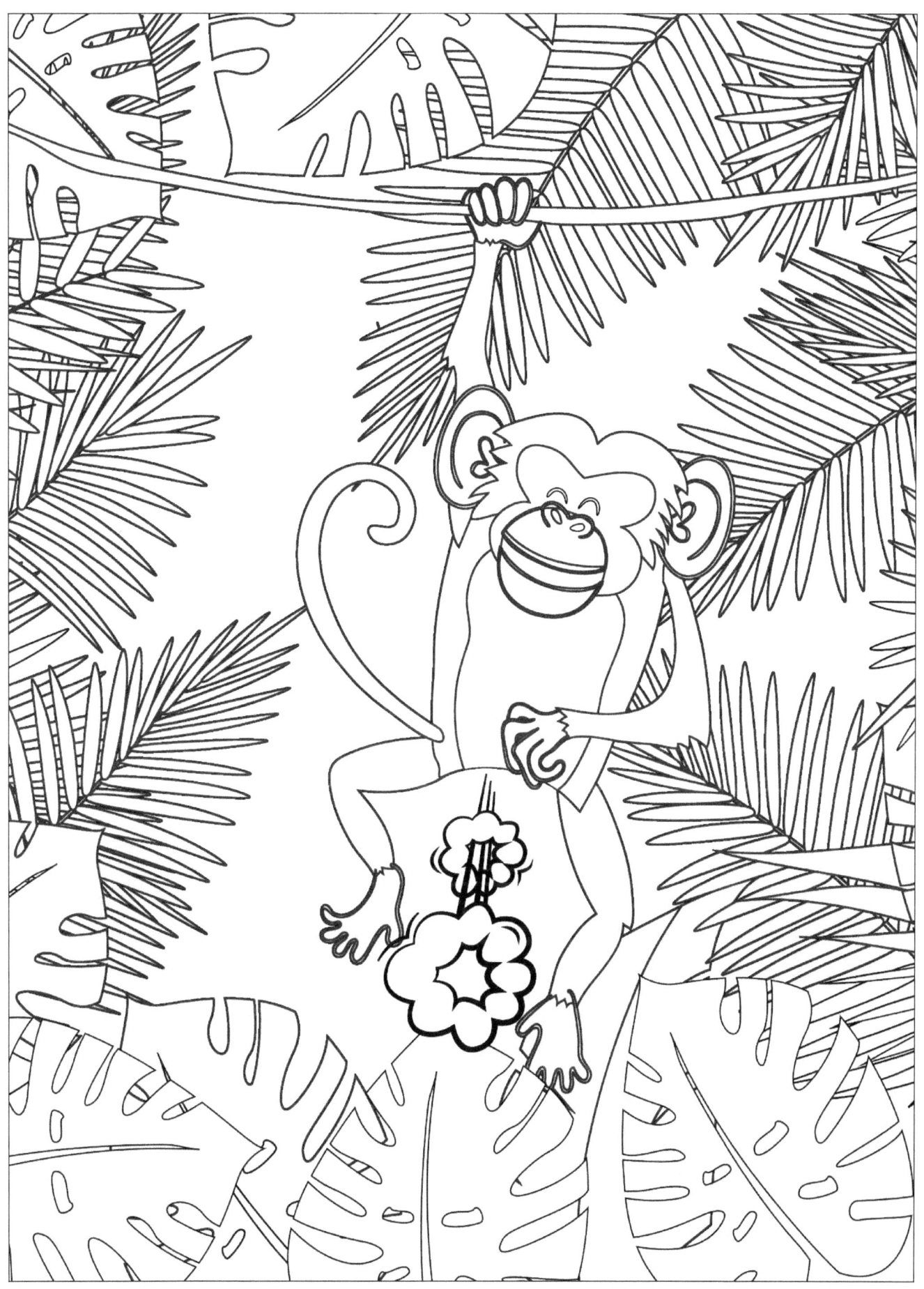

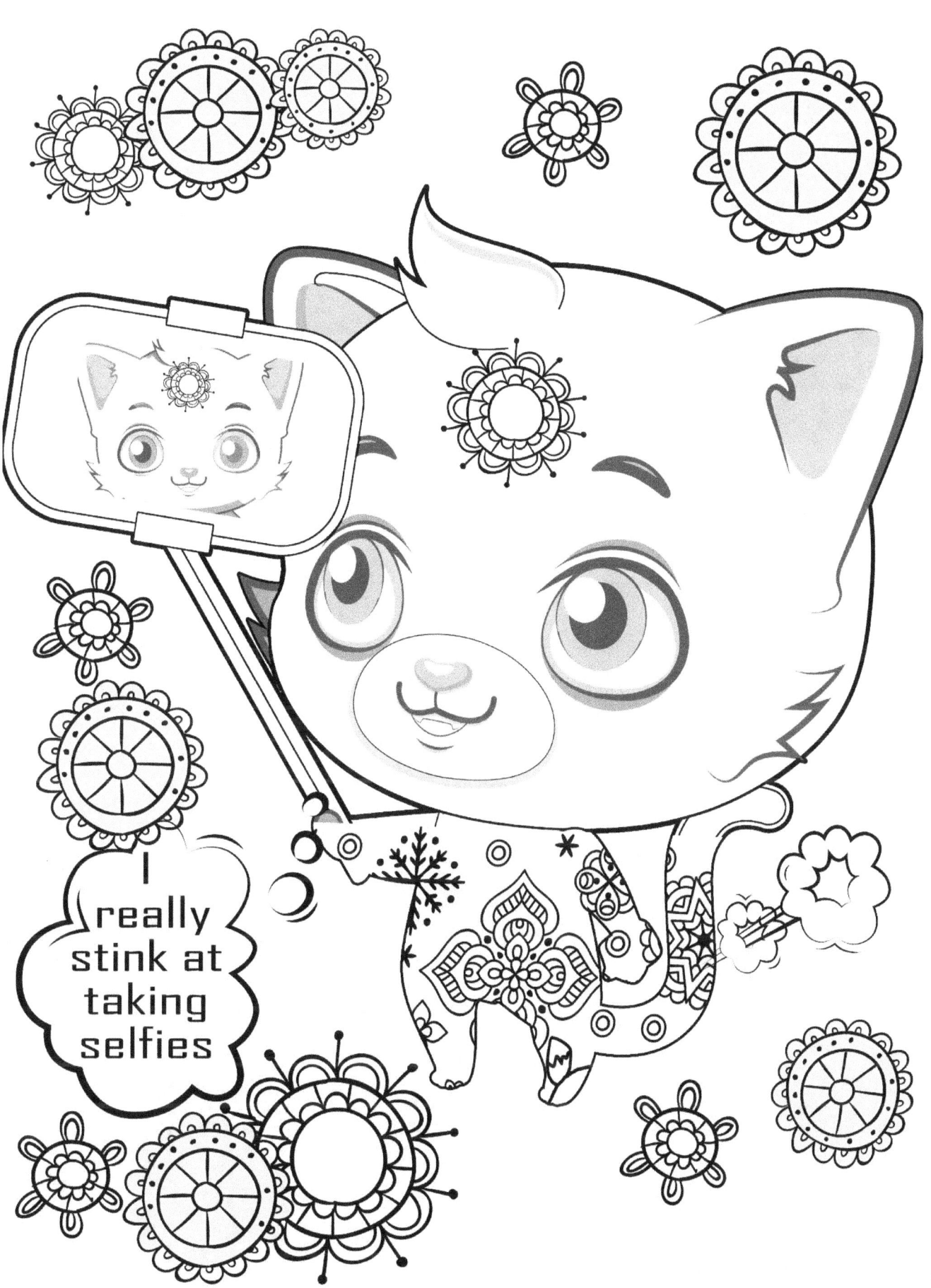

www.ingramcontent.com/pod-product-compliance
Lightning Source LLC
Chambersburg PA
CBHW081255180526
45170CB00007B/2442